It's My Dream... And Who Am I To Stop Me?

A long hard look at who is really responsible for achieving our dreams

Sandy Geroux

ISBN #: Hardcover 0-9788269-0-6

Softcover 0-9788269-1-4

This book was printed in the United States of America.

To order additional copies of this book, please contact:

Geroux Performance Group
1-866-954-2277
www.sandygeroux.com
sandyg@sandygeroux.com

Contents

Purpose of the Book

I knew there was something else I wanted to do.

I could sense it.

I could feel it.

I could *taste* it.

Unfortunately, I didn't believe it.

I *couldn't* believe it.

I spent 15 years not believing I could do more.

Not believing I was capable.

Not believing I'd be given an opportunity.

Not believing I deserved it.

I was wrong.

Through misguided beliefs and low expectations, I inadvertently sabotaged my own success.

From my speaking engagements, I know there are many others doing the same thing. I speak to both adult and youth groups, and whenever I conduct one of my programs on taking risks or setting and achieving goals, I ask them all to share one of their dreams with one or two of their fellow attendees. I then ask for volunteers to share their dreams with the entire group. A very interesting phenomenon invariably occurs at this point.

When I ask youth group attendees who has a dream, not only is every hand in the room raised, but they all nearly jump out of their seats in an effort to get me to call upon them to share their dreams with the entire group. One little boy of about 5 years old (the brother of an award recipient at a banquet at which I was speaking) raised his hand. When I brought the microphone to him, he said, "Um, um, um… I want to go to college!" He was the cutest thing you ever saw as he proudly proclaimed the dream he had to struggle to think up on the spot! Even though he didn't have a dream ready when the question was asked, he instinctively knew that it was so important to have a dream that he just had to be called upon and he would think of one!

On the other hand, whenever I do this exercise with adults and ask them the question: "How many people have a dream?", 40% - 50% of the group do not even raise their hand. Furthermore, when I ask who will actually *share* their dreams with the group, the percentage drops to about 25% - or less!

Something has happened to us along the way from childhood to adulthood. Many of us have lost the ability to dream at all; most of the rest of us who do dare to dream, don't dare to share our dreams with anyone else.

The purpose of this book is to help us realize what's happened to us on our journey from childhood to adulthood. Once we uncover the myths that cause us to stop dreaming (or to share our dreams with others), as well as recognize and eliminate the mindsets and excuses we all use to sabotage our dreams, we can eliminate the barriers to our success.

I don't know how long it's been since you've dared to dream. Please take my advice: don't wait 15 years for your success, as I did… and if it's already been 15 years or more, your time has come.

I hope this book helps you move from sensing it, feeling it, and tasting it to believing it – and finally, to doing it.

Introduction

Dreams are wispy things – tough to grasp, tough to grab and tough to hold onto.

Many people don't dream. Some don't know how to dream. Others have forgotten how. They may have known how to dream as children, but have lost that ability somewhere along the way.

Some don't dare to dream, having learned at an early age the unfortunate (and incorrect) lesson that it's not worth dreaming, or that their dreams probably won't come true anyway, so why bother?

Some dare to dream, but don't dare to put those dreams into words. Still others dream, talk and even write about their dreams, but don't dare act on them for fear of being disappointed when the dream doesn't happen.

You see, many people would rather experience the *hope* that a dream could happen than risk the *reality* that it doesn't. The problem is that their resultant inaction often causes them to leave this world with their dreams unfulfilled anyway.

We have two choices in life. We can either look back upon a life of fulfillment *in spite of* the obstacles we've overcome, or we can look back and try to justify our lack of success. Given the choice, I believe that no matter how good the justification for our failure, every one of us would rather do the former than the latter.

Many people would rather experience the *hope* that a dream could happen than risk the *reality* that it doesn't.

I've had many opportunities to make one choice or the other in my life, as I'm sure you've had in yours. As I reflect back, I realize there were several important points in my journey where the choices I made had a significant impact on the direction of my life, whether or not I realized it at the time.

As we proceed further in this book, I will share many of those moments with you to illustrate the points I make in each chapter. However, the biggest turning point in my professional life came after more than 15 years of excuses, poor justifications for not taking risks and lack of self-confidence.

It was February of 1995. I was in what was to be my final secretarial position, working for a man who apparently believed that "leadership by intimidation" was the way to keep his employees in line. What was worse was that his wife (who didn't work for the company) believed in this philosophy even more passionately than he did, wielding her power as "the boss's wife" in such a way as to cause people to tremble when she walked through the halls of the company.

As her husband's secretary, I was personally in this woman's line of fire and first felt the true power of her wrath after only three weeks in my new job when the person whom I had sent to deliver a piece of correspondence to her home did not deliver it in the fashion she desired. She proceeded to berate me, call me names, ask me how stupid I was and demand to know how *I* could treat her that way, screaming incessantly at me over the telephone for what felt like an eternity. I was stunned!

What had I done? I was an executive secretary with many years of successful experience at large national and international companies where I had been treated as a trusted partner by the Presidents for whom I'd worked. I'd traded a significantly higher-paying job in Boston for this job in order to work closer to home and avoid a lengthy commute through unpredictable winter weather, a job which now had me crying at my desk within three weeks of taking the position. I was 38 years old; I didn't need to be treated this way! But I swallowed my pride, convincing myself that she must simply have had an unbelievably bad day. I also couldn't believe that she had gotten to me so badly that it had caused me to react this way.

Unfortunately, this was not an isolated or rare incident either from her or, as I later discovered, from her husband. This pattern continued over a 10-month period, alternating between times when I was a "great secretary" to times when, according to my boss I was so stupid that, "I knew I never should have trusted you to do this right".

When he uttered those words, after 10 months of almost continual abuse, something inside me snapped. However, in order to fully understand why I withstood those 10 months of abuse, and why I actually "allowed" something inside me to snap at that moment, we must also look at one particular accompanying event that had occurred while this was going on.

In October of 1994, my husband and I had sold our home in Lincoln, RI to buy a smaller condominium on Narragansett Bay in Bristol, RI. Our REALTOR®, Barbara, from whom we'd bought our home in Lincoln 12 years earlier and who sold it for us that October, had also become our friend. Shortly after we bought the condo in Bristol, Barbara made what I assumed was an off-hand comment. She said, "You know, you'd be a good REALTOR®."

I laughed when she said it. Me? I'd never sold a thing in my life! I thanked her for the compliment, and promptly forgot about it. Little did I know that this one sentence had planted a seed in my mind that wasn't about to simply die.

In February of 1995, Barbara repeated the comment to me. Why did she say it again? I'd already informed her that I knew nothing about sales, and had never done that before. Why would she repeat it? Again, I did nothing, but this time my inaction lasted only for a short time, for it was a couple of days later that my boss uttered those fateful words that caused me to snap.

Those words, combined with Barbara's apparent faith in my abilities, made all the difference. When my boss had treated me badly for the previous 10 months, I had allowed it because I truly felt that I had no other options. I was a secretary. What else did I know how to do? Sure, I'd also been a Systems Analyst for four years. While I'd done well in that position, I really didn't want to go back to that career. And when I had ventured into self-employment, I got scared by its immense possibilities and went back to what I knew best (secretarial work) when my mother/business partner needed to leave our business for medical reasons.

But this time, even though I was a secretary, I had the *possibility* to be something else, too. After all, even though I had no faith that I could sell anything, Barbara did have faith in me. In addition, she owned a real estate company; she knew good REALTORS®. If she thought I could do it – and she was willing to give me a chance to prove it – then I had an option!

I allowed Barbara's faith in me to give me faith in myself. I hung onto that faith like a lifeline.

Although I didn't realize it, that "seed" of a comment had obviously been germinating in the back of my brain for months, ever since she'd first said it. Little did my boss (or even I, myself) know that the very next time he treated me with disrespect was going to be his last opportunity to slam me to the ground and expect me to stay there!

When it happened, it occurred over the telephone, and we'd already hung up by the time I fully realized that this was it – this was the turning point: the last time I would take that kind of treatment from him, or anyone else.

I put the phone down. The secretary at the desk next to mine had heard my side of the telephone exchange and knew that he'd done it again. But when I turned to her, she could tell immediately that something was different. She was concerned that I would do something rash. She tried to comfort me. But this time, there were no words to either comfort me or hold me there any longer.

I called my husband and told him what had happened – again. I told him that this was the final straw and I planned to quit. He agreed that this was the best course of action. The decision was made. I hung up the phone, went immediately to the office of the Human Resources Director and told him that my boss had just abused me for the last time. I quit!

We both agreed that it would be best if I just cleaned out my desk and left without notice, for we both knew there would be no way I could continue to work for them once my boss and his wife knew I planned to leave. So, I left…

…and I have never looked back.

I enrolled in real estate school, got my license and began working for Barbara's company. Sure enough, because I had no sales experience and didn't know what I was doing, I made very little money during my first year of sales.

Uh-oh! I'd gone from a job that provided benefits and paid almost $40,000 a year to one in which I worked over 60 hours a week and made only $13,000, with no benefits!

Luckily, my husband and I had been frugal over the years and had not lived beyond our means. We had no credit card debts and no mortgage since we'd paid cash for the condo because we'd down-sized from our bigger home in Lincoln. [By staying in Lincoln for 12 years, we had allowed appreciation to occur and had also paid extra on the mortgage each month to get the principal balance down as low as possible, as quickly as possible.] So, I had support from husband and the financial ability to continue in my new career, even though my income wasn't yet where it needed to be.

Most importantly, once I had found my courage and confidence to take the first big leap, I discovered that it was much easier to continue to have that confidence when the next hurdle arose. Now, instead of saying, "I don't deserve this kind of treatment, but what are my options?" I said to myself, "I'm 38 years old. I haven't failed at a job yet, and I'm not about to start now!" (I did not consider my final secretarial job a failure – quitting that job was self-preservation!)

So, I attended more classes, asked a lot of questions, and discovered that there were coaches who could mentor you and help you succeed more quickly than you'd be able to do on your own. So I continued learning all I could and hired a coach at the end of 1996. In 1997, I earned more money in my sales career than I'd ever earned in any other career I'd ever tried. And in 1998, I broke the 6-figure income barrier for the first time in my life.

THAT changed everything! It changed everything about the way I looked at my potential as an income-earner; it changed the way I viewed my potential as a woman; and most of all, it exemplified to me the fact that I could count on myself to perform, even when the chips were down.

Success is an interesting phenomenon. Before you achieve big success, it's difficult to believe that you actually could achieve it. But the first time you do go out on a limb and achieve the big success you desire, you discover a newfound belief in yourself that makes it easier to try new things in the future.

I discovered that Barbara had been right! I'd been wrong. Just because I'd never tried sales before in my life didn't mean that I could *never* try it and succeed. As silly as it sounds, this had been what I had believed – and my belief that this was true (a.k.a. fear of failure) was so strongly rooted in my mind that I couldn't even allow myself to seriously consider taking new risks. As soon as they appeared, I shut them down with very plausible-sounding excuses and justifications. Once I proved to myself that I could try something completely foreign to me and succeed, I no longer needed to cling to excuses and justifications for not trying something different.

But how do you get past the point of excuses and take action? For me, it took a combination of the following factors – as well as my recognition and (at least subconscious) acceptance of their reality – to get me to take the leap the first time:

- Belief in my abilities (even if it was someone other than myself who held those beliefs)
- Opportunity (Barbara was willing to give me a chance)
- The catalyst (the final insult that resulted in my snapping – the "point of no return")
- The lack of anything standing in my way – there was no one (and no circumstance) that I could blame or use to justify *not* trying to break away this time – no one but myself, that is.

What beliefs do you hold that are keeping you from your true goals and desires? Can you recognize and accept the combination of factors that will allow you to break through your first barrier, allowing other barriers to come tumbling down after that? Are you positioned properly to do so?

You see, it's all a matter of positioning!

- If your mindsets are not in the right position, they'll prevent you from recognizing and accepting the truths that will allow you to succeed.
- If your emotions are not in the right position, they'll prevent you from mustering enough courage to believe in yourself and try something new.
- If your attitude is not positioned properly (possibly because you're not in your dream career yet, so why bother giving this "interim" position your all?), it will prevent you from putting your best foot forward in every situation, causing you to lose the opportunity to prominently display all you're capable of doing.
- If your body is not in the right position – as far away from negative people and influences as possible – it will prevent you from eliminating the excuses that enable you to remain dissatisfied and unfulfilled for a long time.

What's standing in your way – other than yourself?

Once you position yourself at the "point of no return", you will realize – as I did – that after you've eliminated (or at least made a viable plan to eliminate) all tangible barriers to your success (education, experience, finances), the last one is usually the hardest, and it all boils down to – YOU.

Instances of self-sabotage are difficult to recognize and correct, but not impossible. It's time for us to take a long, hard look at who is really stopping us from achieving our dreams. Once you do this, positioning yourself to recognize and capitalize on the existence of factors that will enable you to succeed, the last barrier will fall for you, too.

I had to get past… "myself" and position myself for success.

Will you eliminate your last barrier and get past… "yourself"?

Part I:

Mindsets & Habits

Preface:

It's Not My Fault

a.k.a. Let the Excuses Begin!

We all make unconsciously self-limiting statements (a.k.a. excuses) such as, "Why won't anyone give me a break?" or "I wasn't born into the right circumstances. I'm just not that lucky, so I'll never get a chance to do anything big!"

During 15 years of holding myself back, I frequently used these and a number of other excuses. I always made them sound *really good* – so good they fooled everyone, including myself. I was very creative in finding ways to point the finger anywhere else but at myself. But, as Judge Mathis once said during an interview I had with him, "Whenever you point the finger at someone else, remember that there are three more pointing back at yourself!"

A Society of Placing Blame

While it is only human to ask these types of questions, our society today has become one of playing the "blame game", placing blame on everyone and everything – except ourselves. It's never *our* fault that we do not succeed. It's never *our* fault that opportunity passes us by. It's never *our* fault that we are unable to achieve our dreams.

In fact, in this type of society our fate seems so obviously "out of our hands" that some people move in a disastrous direction, seeking opportunities to "get rich quick" by taking advantage of others.

Headlines abound in which these situations are described. A man without the willpower to avoid fattening foods blames the fast food industry for his weight; a woman without enough common sense to avoid placing a hot drink in her lap while driving blames the company that sold her the beverage; parents reluctant to discipline their children blame schools for not teaching values that should be taught at home. People staging auto accidents and faking injuries to capitalize on the deep pockets of "rich" insurance companies are all-too-common occurrences in a society gone haywire.

The list goes on and on.

These activities are misguided efforts on the part of some to regain a sense of control over their lives and fates.

And society does them no favor by rewarding such behavior. It provides abusers with short-lived rewards, only to leave them just as empty and shallow afterward as they were before, forcing them to continue abusing in order to gain more rewards. It robs responsible citizens of their ability to purchase reasonable services, such as insurance and medical care, due to escalating costs caused by these abuses. Most of all, it frustrates contributing members of society who dream of a better situation, but have a harder and harder time visualizing a way to make it happen.

Sadly, many have simply given up trying for – or even dreaming of – a better reality.

While there is no easy solution to this problem, one remedy is for society to stop rewarding people for placing blame where it doesn't belong while simultaneously punishing those who try to do what's right.

However, although these societal issues are a problem, they will never be resolved until an increasing and less obvious epidemic is corrected. This is the subconscious self-sabotage of well-intended and responsible people who wish to get ahead but allow fear and doubt to stop them. They do this through the creative use of excuses to justify their fears.

Therefore, another remedy is for each of us to eliminate the excuses holding us back and do something to create our own success. Since this remedy is much more within our personal control than the societal one, this area is the focus of this book.

Personal responsibility

If people think about personal responsibility at all, it has become a notion acknowledged **only** when accepting blame for negative actions or circumstances. What is often overlooked is the fact that, in addition to accepting responsibility or blame when necessary, we must also believe we have (and can take) personal responsibility for creating positive circumstances in our lives. After all, if it's possible to cause negative circumstances in our lives, isn't it only logical to assume that we can also cause positive ones to occur?

If it's possible to cause negative circumstances in our lives, isn't it only logical to assume that we can also cause positive ones to occur?

Therefore, in addition to eliminating the excuses holding us back, we all must embrace the necessity and benefit of taking personal responsibility for creating our own positive outcomes, while still accepting personal responsibility for any mistakes we may make along the way.

If it's meant to be, it will be

There's a fine line between trusting that something is meant to be and therefore not forcing an issue versus sitting around waiting for some spectacular event to bring about success in our lives. Too many of us are anxiously awaiting our turn to hit the cosmic lottery. Since we are convinced one must exist for everyone who is wildly successful, we do nothing to actively cause it to happen for ourselves.

If we take this attitude, we may wait forever for something that will never happen. We can't just sit back and wait for good things to come to us. Whether it's inspiration, luck, or fate – we must go out and find it and create our own luck. Whether we take massive action at one point in time or take baby steps for a long time, the *only* way to get to our destination is by taking action. We cannot sit back with the unrealistic expectation that "something good is going to happen for me, somehow – I just know it!" It won't just happen to us – we must make it happen for ourselves. Successful people decide not to wait for something big to happen *to them*. They decide to make something big happen *for themselves.*

Taking a "wait and see what comes to me" attitude can be compared to playing the lottery, complicated by the fact that you haven't bought a ticket. Did you know that the odds of winning the Florida lottery (the state in which I now live) are 1 in 22,957,480? That's bad enough! When you don't even buy a ticket, your odds have just gone down to 0 in 22,957,480!

Do you really want to have the same odds of succeeding in life as those of winning the lottery, even with a ticket? Relying on luck alone makes our chances of winning in life almost as improbable as winning the lottery, even when we do buy a ticket! Without actively making a plan to reach our goals, we must simply rely on luck and that's not a good plan if we really want to succeed.

Gambling on the lottery to financially support ourselves is not a smart move. Neither is doing so with our own fate, gambling away our lives only to find at the end that we've done the wrong things (or we've done nothing at all), waiting for something unrealistic to occur.

In likening achieving success to winning a lottery, many similarities are evident:

Lottery	**Life**
Many people don't play because it's practically futile	Many people figure they may as well not try because they believe it's futile
They wish it could happen, even though they're convinced it won't	They wish they could have more, but are convinced they won't get it
They feel winning's just for the lucky	They feel success is just for the lucky, the blessed, the rich
They feel jealousy toward winners	They feel jealousy toward highly successful people
They feel helpless, powerless to win	They feel helpless, powerless to succeed
They take one action, then wait for success; if they don't	They take one action, then wait for success; if it doesn't happen,

win, they give up, say, "it figures", etc. – or, they repeat this cycle, trying for a lucky break week after week	they make excuses and give up; or even worse, they repeat the same actions over and over, expecting a different outcome (success) next time
We must take action: buy a ticket	We must take action: invest in ourselves
Without buying a ticket, there is NO chance of winning	Without investing in ourselves, there is NO chance of success
The more tickets we buy, the greater the chance of winning	The more we invest in ourselves, the greater the chance of succeeding
Based on luck alone, the odds of winning are not good	Based on luck alone, the odds of succeeding are not good
If we put all our eggs in one basket, we will probably not win	If we put all our eggs in one basket, we will probably not succeed

Please don't get me wrong. I'm not advocating gambling on the lottery with this example! I'm simply trying to prove the point that many similarities exist, and if we're going to gamble on something, it should be on ourselves and our own success – something worthwhile and absolutely within our control!

The lottery is NEVER within our control and yet some people still try to win it. Our lives are completely within our control, yet many people refuse to even *try* to win in this area.

Excuses

I could write an entire book on the excuses and justifications I have heard (and often used, I hate to admit) before, during and after various goal-setting attempts. To focus on this factor in this book, strong emphasis has been placed on identifying them.

To this end, each chapter contains a list of the most popular excuses used to justify the fears surrounding topics in that chapter. I have also provided space for you to write your own "favorite" excuses around those issues, in an effort to help you recognize and eliminate them in the future.

In addition, to move you to action, there is a section that recaps the major points of the chapter, including the myths identified and a section of tips to help move you to take action (the key to success) to begin rectifying the issues you recognize in your own behavior patterns relevant to those topics.

The insidious nature of excuses is that they are based on – and sound dangerously similar to – true and legitimate reasons that sometimes exist for NOT attempting a goal. However, **legitimate reasons** and **excuses** are two very different things. One is a valid reason to take (or not take) a particular action, even to the point of quitting on a particular project before getting in any deeper once you realize you're traveling down an undesirable path; the other is simply what we tell ourselves and others to make us feel better about quitting *without good reason.*

In an effort to recognize the various points in the goal achievement process at which we are vulnerable to (and most likely to use) excuses, let's look at three categories of excuses.

Excuses before the fact:

These are the excuses that prevent us from trying anything new. Excuses such as the following are common at this stage:

"I don't know what I want to do"

"I don't know how to do that"

"I'm afraid to do that."

"What if I fail?"

"No one else is doing that/has ever done that"

"I can't do that! I'm not smart/rich/good enough to do that"

"I've never done that before."

"It's always been done this way!"

By thinking up multitudes of reasons NOT to do things, we successfully avoid ever finding real reasons TO do them, thus "preventing" ourselves from failing. Of course, we also prevent ourselves from ever trying or succeeding at anything new and different in the process...

Just because you're not sure of EXACTLY what you want to do, don't let it stop you from doing *something*. Most of us don't know exactly what we want to do right from the start. We normally begin with something we know, that we're comfortable with, or something in which an opportunity has arisen. For example, I started as a secretary because it was something with which I was familiar and comfortable. The problem arose only when I did nothing to achieve my true desires once I decided that my first career wasn't fulfilling them.

Begin by doing something in which you have an interest. Once you begin something, you'll discover if you really do like it (and if you have a talent for it). If not, you can look for other opportunities.

No one is born knowing *how* to do what they want to do. We must learn everything in life, from walking and talking to building a career.

Once you determine what you want to do, there are several things you can do to find out *how* to do it, including:

- Enrolling in adult education classes that teach the skill you need;
- Looking for others who are doing what you want to do, and asking them how they began. They may even volunteer to mentor you;
- Joining associations that specialize in your chosen industry;
- Reading "how-to" books;
- Looking for a job or apprenticeship in your chosen, or a related, field.

There are plenty of resources available that teach the skills necessary to accomplish your goals, once you determine what they are.

Excuses during the fact:

These are the excuses that allow us to justify quitting halfway through a new project. The need for instant (or at least very quick) gratification is so strong that we feel justified in abandoning any new project that takes longer than expected. Unfortunately, this holds true, even when our up-front expectations were unreasonable in the first place! The following excuses are common at this stage:

"Forget it! This is stupid! It isn't working; I know it will never work!"

"I can't do this – it's too hard!

"This is taking too long!"

"I'm not good at this!"

"I don't have enough money to do this!"

"I don't have time for this!"

"No one ever told me it would be like this!"

Having these excuses handy helps us feel better about quitting when a goal becomes difficult to achieve, even when we really want to accomplish it. We use these excuses to justify our reasons for quitting, in order to give ourselves permission to quit on our goals.

What we must keep in mind is that obstacles are inevitable. In fact, they're often necessary to help us avoid big (or bigger) mistakes in the future. What reasonable person truly expects to succeed at everything we try, the very first time we try it? When we reason it out, no one really expects this to happen. Yet, we're constantly surprised when it does happen! We must stop setting ourselves up for failure by holding unreasonable expectations up front.

Don't look at obstacles as excuses to stop; view them as opportunities to learn and grow, and to become more effective at achieving the rest of your goals in the future.

Excuses after the fact:

These are the excuses we use to make ourselves feel better once we have already quit on a project or goal. By convincing ourselves and others that the goal wasn't really a true goal, we can feel better about the fact that we didn't achieve it.

This also helps us believe that we really didn't make a half-hearted effort (even if we did). We convince ourselves that we just knew, deep-down, that it wasn't for us. That's why the dedication, effort and commitment weren't there – simply because "my heart wasn't in it." Excuses that include the following are common at this stage:

"I didn't really want to do that anyway!"

"I told you I was no good at this!"

"I never should have tried this; I never should have listened to you!"

"Well, if I'd had any luck at all, this would have worked."

Do you recognize any of these excuses? I know I do; that's how I could think of so many! Until we recognize what we're doing to sabotage our own goals, we will never achieve the success we desire. I hope the excuses we've just demonstrated, as well as others that follow in this book, help you uncover the ways you sabotage your dreams, and help you recognize and eliminate them in future goal-setting efforts.

The human factor

In addition to breaking down into categories the excuses we use, we must also analyze and recognize the fears and human factors that actually prevent our success. They fall into the following major categories (listed along with their associated common excuses):

Procrastination:

I'll do that, as soon as this is done

I'll start that on Monday/after the holiday/when I have more time

Perfectionism:

I'll get to it when all my materials are perfect

As soon as I get ALL my ducks in a row (which never happens because we always find another "duck" that needs to be put into the row), I'll start that project

This is not the perfect time to try that right now

Fear of Failure:

What if I don't succeed?

No one's ever done that before

Lots of people have tried that before, and they haven't succeeded – what makes me think I can do it?

I don't have enough money

I'm not smart enough

I'm not good enough

Fear of Rejection:

What if I they say no?

What if they yell at me/are nasty to me?

What if they slam the door in my face/refuse to see me or talk to me?

What if they hang up on me?

Fear of Success:

What if I succeed and people realize it was a fluke/an accident?

What if I don't really belong there?

How do I stay on top?

What would I do if I ever did accomplish that? I'd be terrified!

Fear of Embarrassment:

I'll be so embarrassed if I try and fail!

What we're forgetting is that we already fail simply by NOT trying. We're also fooling ourselves into believing that others don't recognize this. Other people do recognize it. The only difference between reality and perception is that our embarrassment is not there because we simply don't acknowledge the fact that we're not doing what we want to do.

If we become more self-aware, we'll enable our success and the resulting recognition from others. Keeping ourselves "in the dark" about our lack of success doesn't make it any less real.

Determining if we're using excuses or true reasons

So, if our minds are really that tricky, and we are able to so easily convince ourselves that we should quit, even when we shouldn't, how do we determine when a true reason exists to give up on a goal or dream?

I have found that using the following questions and criteria have been helpful to me in determining whether or not I'm simply giving up on a goal or legitimately "stopping the bleeding":

1. Is this goal something that I really do want to do? Have I wanted to do it over a long time? Has that goal not changed over time?
2. Do I feel sad or wistful whenever I see someone else accomplishing this same goal? Do I envy them – and wish it were me?
3. If I could make just three wishes that were guaranteed to come true, would this be one of them?
4. Is there another way I can incorporate this activity/function/dream into an existing career or life activity? (For example, I am a singer. I may not ever make it as a solo artist, but when I discovered that I loved and missed singing once I began my speaking career because I had no time for it, I decided to incorporate it into my speaking career. Now, I'm thrilled and fulfilled – and my audiences love the addition of music to my programs.)
5. Do I have the talent and ability to do what I want to do? If I recognize legitimate limitations, how can I utilize the talents I do have to best advantage and fulfill this dream in another

manner? (Painters without the use of their hands who paint magnificent works of art by holding the paintbrush between their teeth or their toes leap to mind here.)

6. If I really can't fulfill my original dream, can I find and fulfill a different dream I never before realized was possible?

The answers to these questions depend on you – and on your desires. Don't deny a dream just because it's difficult to achieve. However, don't chase a dream simply because you're too stubborn to admit something has changed, or you've come to the realization that you're holding yourself back from realizing other dreams by the single-minded pursuit of an unreasonable one.

If we simply get rid of the excuses, listen to the legitimate reasons for doing (or not doing) things, and admit our dreams, we can prepare ourselves for what must be done to accomplish them… rather than later in life having to justify why we have never quite been happy.

Structure of this book

This book is divided into three sections. The first section contains chapters that include the mindsets and concepts, as well as a gray-colored section at the end of each chapter containing:

- an Overview of the Myths to Bust (those addressed in the chapter as well as your own);
- a list of the most common excuses used to justify the fears addressed in the chapter (the most common excuses as well as your own);
- a list of Key Concepts containing tips for taking action

The first section deals with mindsets and recognizing our current behavior patterns, attitudes and thinking, in an effort to uncover whether they are productive or harmful to achievement of our goals.

The second contains everyday success stories that have inspired me, in the hope that they will also inspire you and help you realize that they abound everywhere – not just in the newspapers and on television! You may even be one yourself…

The third section is a brief reminder that we must leave a legacy of hope in our wake so future generations grow up with as much hope and promise as those in the past.

So let's move forward because, after all…

It's Your Dream…And Who Are You To Stop You?

Chapter One

But I Do Want Success!

a.k.a. Desire is Not the Same As Motivation

The Myth of Desire vs. Motivation

We all *desire* success, whether in the form of love, financial wealth, fame, fortune or something altogether different. Some people talk a good game, always planning big things, even "bragging" about who and what they know and how wonderful everything will be, but never quite muster enough energy, vision or perseverance to get the job done. Successful people are willing to work hard for success, putting their money and energy where their mouth is.

This is where motivation comes into play. Motivation comes from within. It is the force that drives to us action in order to achieve our goals. It is an inner strength, the will to succeed that comes into play when we encounter obstacles, fear and frustration. It is what separates those who intend to succeed (but never do) from those who persevere and accomplish their dreams.

Motivation does not come from other people. Other people's successes, actions and/or words may inspire us, but they cannot motivate us to do anything we don't really want to do; nor can they motivate us to begin or complete anything if we don't have sufficient motivation from within to see it through. This is why nagging, preaching, crying and other tactics do not work when anyone attempts to get someone else to do a task they really don't want to do.

I have learned this in coaching sessions with clients. I now screen my coaching clients very carefully, lest I waste their time and mine, or falsely lead them to believe I can externally motivate them to succeed. They must already possess inner drive and motivation, or it will not work. I can certainly inspire them with lessons I've learned and successes I've achieved. I can also help them avoid the mistakes I've made. I can even give them tools and techniques I've used, mindsets and scripts for business and life, and creative ideas to help them grow and be successful.

But neither I nor anyone else can motivate them to actually achieve their goals if they are not willing – and more importantly, committed – to doing so themselves.

The Myth of the Self-Starter

Many people are self-starters. They draw from a pool of inner resources to begin the steps toward their goals, believing that if they have enough drive to start a project, they will finish it.

> **It's simply not enough to be a self-starter. We must be a self-completer as well.**

This is where the myth of being a self-starter sabotages our success. It's simply not enough to be a self-starter. We must be a "self- completer," as well. Most of us can start a project with the best of them. Completing it is an entirely different story, as we encounter obstacles along the way that require perseverance in order to achieve what we desire.

Look around your home (or garage). How many projects have you begun that are half-done, one-quarter done, even 99% done – but are not quite finished yet? How many works-in-process clutter your home or office, or both? These are projects that were once so exciting (or necessary) that you started them with anxious anticipation of how great the final result would be.

So, what happened? What could cause a new and exciting project to come to a screeching halt?

External and Internal Factors That Stop Us

Usually it's a combination of factors, rather than one isolated reason, that cause us to abandon – or postpone – a project.

There are factors **external** to ourselves, including:

- Ease and/or convenience of fixing the current problem
- The expense of the "fix"
- The necessity of the finished project

In some cases, we realize halfway through the project that we need another part, tool, or supply we don't have on hand. Or, a necessary item on the Parts List is missing and we have to wait for it to be shipped to us before we can put together the toy or piece of furniture we've just purchased!

If it's just a case of needing something we can easily pick up at the store, we plan to get it. Whether we actually do make it back to the store or not often depends on the expense of the needed item, as well as the necessity of the finished product. For example, if we're putting together a bed frame and cannot finish creating a comfortable place to sleep without additional materials, we will feel a strong urgency to go to the store, purchase the item, and complete the project.

However, if we're building a new china cabinet, we may not feel the same sense of urgency to return to the store immediately to purchase needed supplies, especially if the store is not conveniently located.

The result may be that, depending on the absolute necessity of the finished product (or lack thereof), the absence of an item costing all of $1.75 could cause us to sabotage our good intentions to finish a project!

On the other hand, sometimes a lack of expertise or instruction stops us. I can't count how many crocheting projects I started when I was a teenager, but never finished because Grandma only showed me how to *start* them (to get me going), but we never got back together for the lesson on how to *finish* them! Combine this with the fact that I was not *intensely* interested in crocheting, nor did I have a burning need for crocheted items in my home, and the result is that I have never taken the time to learn how to finish my crocheting projects.

While all of the above factors are valid and of varying degrees of difficulty to correct, the more difficult factor to correct is **internal**, and it all boils down to our persistence in the face of large or small obstacles. It is:

- Our own sheer determination, combined with
- Our desire for success in that area

We may just give it up because it wasn't that important to us anyway (or so we'd like to claim once we've decided to quit partway through the project). Or, it may become a "battle of wills" between the unfinished project and our self-satisfaction.

We often joke about our "works of art" or "masterpieces in process" (more often, our significant others joke about them for us), but these items serve as constant reminders of our failure to complete project after project, littering our lives with the decaying "corpses" of half-finished endeavors and half-baked ideas we never return to once we've left them. These barebones skeletons seem to mock us, serving only to de-motivate us from trying any more new projects, lest we waste even more time and money providing additional fodder for our guests to joke about at our next dinner party!

The solution to finally dealing with the existing half-finished projects cluttering your life is this: get rid of them or finish them! I know it's difficult to throw away something you've spent time and money trying to complete, but if you're never going to finish it anyway, the time and money are already spent and gone! Keeping the project around the house will not bring them back. The first – and hardest – step is admitting that you will never get around to finishing the project. Once you've made that determination, the next steps will be much easier.

One way or the other, make a positive difference in your life and your attitude by getting rid of the junk cluttering your life and preventing you from moving forward.

Going forward, a better solution is to avoid these types of problems in the first place by following a few simple guidelines:

- Plan ahead whenever you decide to tackle a new project. Accumulate all necessary tools, equipment and money up front. Make a checklist of what you will need, and how much it will cost.
- Acquire the knowledge necessary not only to start the project, but to complete it as well!
- Read the directions – **first** (I can't recall how many projects have taken me three times as long to complete than they would have taken if I had just read the directions first!)
- Ask for help from willing friends and loved ones.

Armed with the tools, knowledge and other resources you need, you can begin and complete projects in as little time, and with as little effort, as possible.

Nourishment for our happiness in life

Imagine going into the kitchen to prepare dinner without having any food on hand, or cooking a meal only halfway through. Not only would a half-cooked meal taste terrible, but it may actually be unhealthy. What would happen if you continued to half-cook your meals? If you didn't die of starvation first, you could hurt or kill yourself with food poisoning.

Just as food is nourishment for the physical body, we must view the achievement of goals as nourishment for our happiness and attitude in life, taking care to give our attitude the right nourishment or it will die – taking all our hopes and dreams with it.

Just as food is nourishment for the physical body, we must view the achievement of goals as nourishment for our happiness and attitude in life.

Our varying levels in nourishing our attitudes explain why different people react differently upon meeting someone who has achieved their dreams:

- Some are jealous
- Some act indifferent or scoff at the other person's success (which is likely another indicator of jealousy)
- Some are truly happy for those who have achieved their dreams
- Some allow the other person's success to inspire them to do the same
- Some truly don't desire success (an especially sad statement since it means these people have given up hope in a society overflowing with opportunity)

Think about it. If your hunger is satisfied, you will not be envious of someone else's lunch. Their enjoyment of their own food will not cause you any discomfort at all. However, if you're starving, you cannot possibly enjoy watching someone else savor a meal. With every bite, hunger gnaws at you, causing you to want what the other person has, because your body *needs* food!

The same happens with your emotional satisfaction. If you're not happy with your life, it is much more difficult to witness the success of others without feeling anger, jealousy and resentment toward them. Once we fill our own bellies, we don't crave the food of others. Likewise, once we fill our own emotional needs, there is no need to be jealous of other people's success.

My husband and I have always had a goal to own our house free and clear, a goal we achieved in 1994. Maybe you have a similar goal. One of my coaching clients once told me that it truly inspired him to hear that when we planned our move to Florida in the year 2000, we had originally intended to finance a small portion of the home we bought there. However, since the closing costs were too high (considering the small amount we wished to finance), we decided to just pay cash for the house. He took heart in knowing that if we could get ourselves into a position to be able to make that kind of financial decision, he could, too.

I don't know what will spark you, but I hope that something you read in this book will inspire you to find your own motivation to achieve your goals.

What spurs you to action? Is it seeing examples of others just like you succeed beyond their wildest dreams? Is it envisioning what life would be like if you were doing what you really wanted to do? Perhaps it is a fear of never being able to provide for your family (or yourself) the things you need to be comfortable and safe?

Whatever it is, look for it all around you. There are many examples of people in your daily life who are living their dreams, and who can serve as examples and encouragement for you.

And don't forget: goal-setting doesn't have to stop with the accomplishment of one goal. After all, no one ever said we're limited to one dream per lifetime! So dream big and dream often!

Myths to bust:

Overview

Myth #1:
Desire and motivation are the same thing.

Myth #2:
Self-starters are guaranteed to achieve their dreams.

What myths do I buy into?

____

____

____

How can I bust them?

____

____

____

Most common excuses we
use to justify our fears and inactivity:

- I really didn't want to do that, anyway!
- I don't have enough time!
- I don't have enough money!
- I can't find/get the stuff I need to finish!
- I don't know how to do that – I've never done it before!

My "favorite" excuses used to justify my fears and inactivity:

Tips to overcome fear and take action:

1) Before beginning a project:
    - Plan ahead whenever you decide to tackle a new project. Accumulate all necessary tools, equipment and money up front. Make checklists with associated budgets.
    - Acquire the knowledge necessary not only to start the project, but to complete it as well.
    - Read the directions – first!
    - Ask for help from willing friends and loved ones.

2) If you've stopped in the middle of a project, determine:
    - The ease and/or convenience of fixing the current problem
    - The expense of the "fix"
    - The necessity of the finished project
    - Your determination and desire to complete that particular project

3) Once you've determined all of the above, either:
    - Finish it! ***OR***
    - Get rid of it!

4) Whenever you feel resentment or jealousy toward someone, look to your own life to find where you may be lacking satisfaction and fulfillment. Once you satisfy your own emotional needs, there will be no need for negative feelings toward the success of others.

Chapter Two

Waiting for the Big Break

a.k.a. Start Making Great Everyday Choices

The Myth of the Big Break

"My big break is coming, and when it does, you just watch me. I'm going straight to the top!" How many times have you heard (or said) these words? They are sometimes uttered by those who are actively looking for that break as well as performing their own actions to progress toward their dreams.

However, they are often spoken by people who haven't positioned themselves to benefit from the break, even if it came along! From teens who say they want to be big sports stars (but don't play sports), to those who want to be famous singers, musicians or actors (but have never written a song and don't practice daily to improve their vocal, acting or technical ability on an instrument), to adults who say they want to progress at their jobs or go into business for themselves (but never go back to school or develop a marketable idea upon which to base a successful business), many people are simply hoping for a big break to stumble across their path rather than trying to put themselves into a reasonable path where a break could actually find them.

I did this for years! I steadfastly hoped for a big break to come along while completely ignoring all the opportunities to capitalize on small breaks that came my way. By failing to recognize the small breaks and opportunities, and by making excuses as to why I couldn't take advantage of that "at that moment," I threw away many opportunities to create my own big break, or at least to allow a big break to come my way by placing myself in a position that enabled me to catch it.

From my desire to be a professional singer (on which I never acted) to my desire to own a big business, to my real estate and speaking careers (which I did capitalize upon and make very successful), I did not become successful until I learned to recognize whatever opportunities came my way and act upon them.

People who doggedly cling to the belief that their "big break" is coming, while doing nothing to help themselves in the meantime, waste their entire lives waiting for this one event by justifying inactivity with a string of excuses because the "right thing" hasn't yet come along. What they don't realize is that if they would only take action in a direction with a definite purpose, they would most likely create their own "breaks" (big and small) that would eventually lead them to success.

Enormous success in life is not usually the result of one giant decision made at one momentous "turning point" in our lives. Rather, it is the result of hundreds of small decisions made on a daily basis, all of which help build (or destroy) a happy and fulfilled life over time.

Many of us make life-altering decisions on a daily basis but fail to recognize a pattern of making the wrong decisions at *seemingly unimportant* but crucial times.

Although no single event of great importance may have happened in our lives, nor has some great tragedy occurred, we continue to make crucial decisions every day that affect the quality of our lives and the lives of those around us. When we forget that we make life-altering decisions on a daily basis and fail to recognize a pattern of making the wrong decisions at *seemingly unimportant* but crucial times, our lives are ruined just as effectively as if we allowed a great and obvious tragedy to do it for us.

If we fail to recognize this concept ourselves, and fail to teach it to our children, we perpetuate the myth that there are only three categories of people who will achieve great things in life:

1) Those born to great wealth and/or circumstances;
2) Those who are tragically affected in some way and are strong enough to survive and thrive afterward; or
3) Those who are just plain lucky (and get that big break).

We must remember (and stress to our children) the negative impact of making the wrong decisions, as well as the positive and continuing impact of making the right ones, especially those necessary in difficult situations.

Today's youth face greater and greater obstacles at very young ages. Drugs, sex and violence play too great a part in our children's lives. The decisions they must make on a daily basis will affect them for the rest of their lives – that is, if they don't destroy their lives before they've really had a chance to begin to live them.

So, why is it so difficult to realize and remember that small everyday decisions and actions affect our lives?

It's because we can't always see the effect that actions performed today will have on our lives tomorrow. This is especially true for children and teens, who do not yet have the life experience necessary to analyze the future consequences of their immediate actions. This is why it's so important for us to guide our children, and remain involved in their lives. Only by being involved can we help them make the right decisions as situations that require good judgment arise.

In addition, by being examples of good judgment ourselves we show our children how our daily actions affect our entire lives. In fact, bad judgment on our part also teaches them the negative consequences of bad decisions. When these situations occur, we must admit our mistakes, find ways to correct them and then go on, in order to teach our children how to recover from the inevitable mistakes they will make in their lives. This also proves to them that most mistakes are not fatal, and that we can fully recover and learn from them.

In Chapter 5, we'll take a closer look at cause and effect. For now, let's take a look at the behavior patterns and choices available to us within the realm of success and failure when trying to accomplish a goal.

Fail/Succeed Behavior Patterns

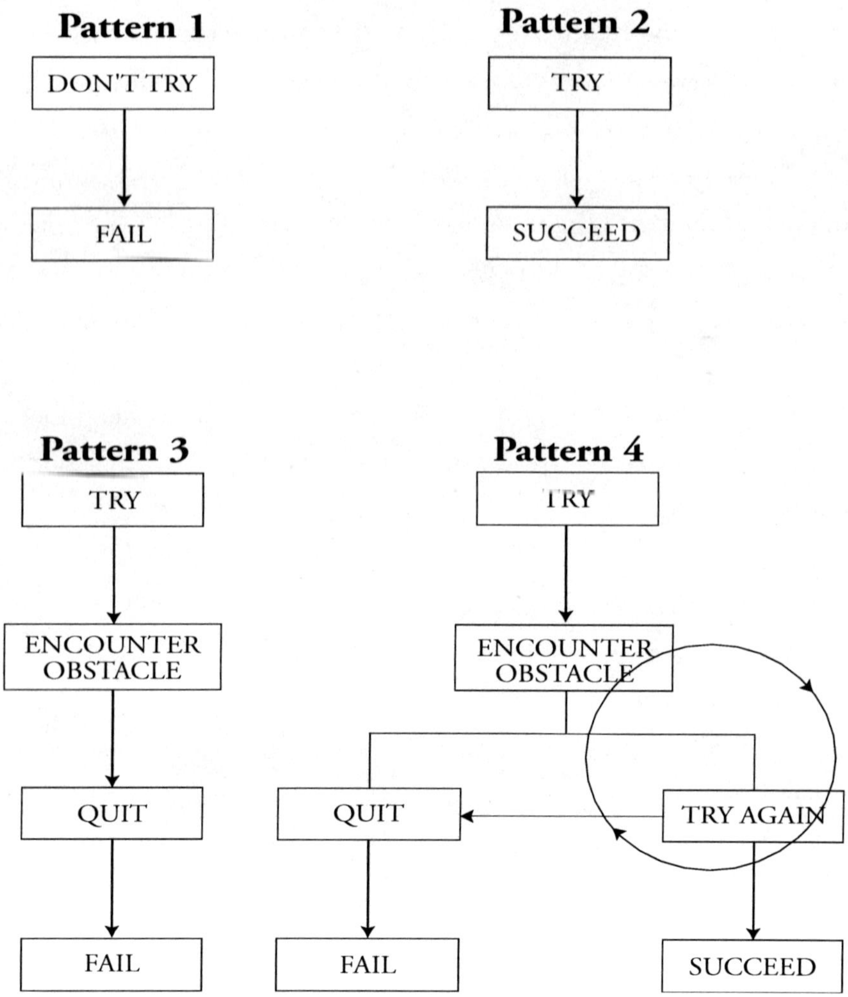

Notice that we always have choices to make along the way.

In **Pattern 1 (Don't Try → Fail)**, it is impossible to miss the fact that if we choose not to even try to reach our goal, we will automatically fail. Is this a pattern of your life? Do you constantly have good ideas, but slam them down without serious consideration? Do you seek excuses to avoid attempting to achieve your dreams in the first place? If so, you must recognize and break out of this pattern, or it will continue to hold you back.

I was stuck in this pattern for the better part of 15 years. Oh, "I tiptoed" out and tried Pattern 3 periodically, but due to my low expectation level and my lack of confidence in my ability to do things I'd never previously seen anyone else I knew do, as soon as the first obstacle came along, I came up with VERY creative excuses to justify not venturing into new waters – excuses that sounded so plausible and so "real" that I not only fooled everyone around me, but I fooled myself into believing they were legitimate, too. My personal *favorite* (for lack of a better term) is this:

At one point, my mother and I had built a successful desktop publishing business. However, it had gotten bigger than she had anticipated (she was just about at retirement age by this time) and she needed knee replacement surgery that would have put her out of commission for quite a while. In addition, once she recovered, at her age Mom didn't want (or need) to resume the level of work we had reached; however, I was relatively close to the beginning of my working career, with no plans or ability to retire for many years.

I was at a crossroad. The idea of buying her out, continuing on my own and opening my own temporary agency in RI came to me as a result of numerous requests we had received for such services in our desktop publishing business. The demand was there, our reputation was there, and very few agencies existed to fill this need in RI at this time. The timing was right! I, however, was not ready. I'd never run a big business before, and this had the potential to be BIG!

A million excuses came to mind. I selected the most plausible-sounding ones to stop myself from taking this risk. Here are my top two: *"I'd have to take on a partner in order to do this, and you know how partnerships never work out!"* and *"My biggest client is in Boston, MA, so how could I open a business in RI with my big client in Boston?"* Mind you, Boston was a mere 40 miles away – less than an hour via major highways! I am absolutely sure I could have found someone to take my place at our Boston client's office, freeing me to run the business. However, my fear of doing something completely new and different, without anyone to guide or encourage me in this new area, stopped me before I could even give it serious consideration.

Whenever I look at the successful temporary agencies that exist now in Providence, RI, I think about the fact that "that could have been me." Don't let this be you; don't defeat your own good ideas without giving them serious consideration regarding whether they actually have a chance to succeed.

In **Pattern 2 (Try → Succeed)**, we try and succeed on our first attempt. While this does occasionally happen, it is extremely rare. However, let's remember that what seems to be Pattern 2 (a.k.a. the "overnight success") is usually not what it appears to be. Usually the person who appears to achieve Pattern 2 really did not become an overnight success, but worked long and hard in anonymity to get to that point. Once they reached the pinnacle, their success came to light, but the hard work that got them there remains hidden from the vast majority, thus creating the myth of the overnight success.*

*Remember that even overnight successes whose success has nothing to do with their own efforts (e.g., heirs and heiresses) have reached their station in life due to the efforts of others who came before them. However, because they did not work hard for their "success", these people are often more harmed than helped by that easy success because they never learn the importance of working for what they want. How many wealthy and/or famous children experience terrible problems stemming from their lack of ability to appreciate hard work or demonstrate personal responsibility? The first time they attempt something on their own, their unrealistic expectations of how easy it will be (combined with the unfortunate but inevitable public scrutiny of their activities) cause them to quit, often resulting in destructive activities designed to hide their pain and embarrassment.

Those who begin their dreams with visions of Pattern 2 in mind are often the ones who quit after they encounter the first obstacle, because their initial expectations are so unreasonable that they have already doomed their efforts at success. When the unreasonable expectation is not fulfilled, the dreamer assumes the dream is impossible to achieve and quits, thus failing by the very act of quitting, resulting in Pattern 3.

Also, those who have experienced an instance of Pattern 2, at least once in their lives, become very disenchanted when that pattern doesn't repeat itself on the next goal they try to achieve. The easy success of the first goal creates the unreasonable expectation that all future successes will come as easily, creating a dangerous precedent that enables Pattern 3 to occur much more quickly in later attempts.

In **Pattern 3 (Try → Encounter Obstacle → Quit → Fail)**, an attempt is made to reach our goal, but we give up when we encounter obstacles (many of us give up after only one try), resulting in failure to achieve the goal.

Pattern 4 adds to **Pattern 3 (Try → Encounter Obstacle → Quit → Fail)** the magical key, the "success step": Persistence **(Try Again → Encounter Obstacle → Try Again → Succeed)**. In other words, we often encounter obstacles that cause us to fail at our initial attempts, and must try again and again to reach our goal. This is the most common (and successful) method of achieving a goal, especially if the goal is large and/or long-term.

Pattern 4 also recognizes that there are numerous opportunities for us to quit along the way, when more than one obstacle is encountered. At any point in this process, if we decide to quit, we fail. Even if we've resisted quitting several times, we must remain vigilant against the temptation to quit after multiple obstacles are encountered. **Persistence** is the key that opens the door to success!

It's important to note here that **persistence** does not mean stubbornness or foolishness in the face of adversity along the way toward achieving a goal. A case in point is that of those brave souls who try again and again to reach the summit of Mt. Everest, or make the long and dangerous journey across Antarctica. They may abandon a particular trip during their quest for that goal, but do not abandon the goal altogether. Especially in life-or-death cases, it's critically important to know the difference between abandoning a particular *step* toward a goal and abandoning the entire goal itself. Making a prudent decision to "live to fight another day" – while it may feel like a gigantic step backward at the time – actually enables them to reach the goal at a later date.

Likewise, we must remember that our goals are not set in stone. Life changes, we change, circumstances change – and what once was a driving goal for us may no longer be so as life unfolds. It's also important to recognize when a dream has moved, shifted or eliminated itself altogether from its original importance in our lives – but we must be careful to do so without simply using *life* as an excuse to give up on a dream that's still meaningful to us.

That's the way life is. Success is not usually handed to us on a silver platter. We must work harder for some dreams than others. (I know, WORK is a four-letter word, but it's one of the few good ones out there!)

Once we recognize our choices as patterns of behavior, we can see which pattern we fit. If our normal pattern is a destructive one, full of unreasonable expectations, we can recognize and change it. If it's a constructive one, we can continue to achieve success and be vigilant against a destructive pattern change.

By working toward our dreams, realizing from the start that it probably won't be an easy road and that there will be obstacles along the way from which we can learn and grow, we can begin a process that will give us a much better chance of persisting until we reach that goal.

Overview

Myths to bust:

Myth #1:

I need to wait for my "big break" to come along before I can get on my way toward achieving my dreams.

Myth #2:

There are only three categories of people who will achieve great things in life:

1. Those born to great wealth and/or circumstances;
2. Those who are tragically affected in some way and are strong enough to survive and thrive afterward; or
3. Those who are just plain lucky (and get that big break).

Myth #4:

The overnight success really does exist.

What myths do I buy into?

How can I bust them?

Most common excuses we
use to justify our fears and inactivity:

- When that big break comes along, then I'll be ready to go!
- No one will give me a break!
- I'm just not that lucky!
- I wasn't born with a silver spoon in my mouth!

My "favorite" excuses used to justify my fears and inactivity:

Tips to overcome fear and take action:

1. Stop whenever you hear yourself saying, "That's a great idea, but…" or "I'd really like to do that, but…". Use the word "but" as a **trigger word** to generate a new response in yourself to analyze whether the thought after that word is legitimate. If so, think about whether there's a way around it or if it really is a showstopper. If there's a way around it, start doing something about it. If not, go on to a goal you can – and should – accomplish.
2. Make a list of pros and cons of the action you're contemplating. See if there are any showstoppers in the "Con" list. If not, begin making a plan to accomplish the dream.
3. Once you decide you want to attempt the dream, begin writing a plan that contains action steps, deadlines and budgets.
4. Gather input from those you know and trust, as well as those with experience and/or expertise in the topic under consideration. Bounce your idea off them. If the majority think it's a bad idea (and have *legitimate* reasons why this is so), brainstorm to see if there's a way to fix whatever problems exist with the issue. If not, go on to a new idea.

Note: Don't be afraid to approach someone who doesn't know you, but who has a great reputation and broad experience in the area of expertise you wish to investigate. You may be surprised to learn how many successful people are willing to help strangers brave enough to reach out and ask for their advice. They may not act as your "personal mentor," but they will likely be able to point you in the right direction, and be happy to answer periodic questions as you travel on your path to success.

Chapter Three

What If I Don't Make It?

a.k.a. It's Not All Just A Big Waste of Time!

A young student in one of my goal-setting seminars once asked me the following question, which illustrates the fear that many people, young and old alike, have of even daring to dream: "What if I try for my dream and don't achieve it? Then I feel like I will have **wasted** all that time trying to get there, only to fail at the end."

While this is a good question, let's look at it objectively.

First of all, trying to achieve any worthwhile goal is never a waste of time, whether or not we eventually succeed. There is always something to be learned along the way.

Secondly, although we may be trying for a certain goal, this doesn't mean that everything else in our lives is put on hold while we try for that one thing. Let's not forget to enjoy our lives as we attempt to achieve our goals.

Third, goals are not static things. As we try to achieve a goal, something may happen to change our goal or our attitudes toward achieving that particular goal. Life changes, we change, our desires change. We may discover an entirely different goal that is much more attractive to us as we grow and mature. We must continually pay attention to what draws our interest, utilizes our talents, and creates a passion within us. Don't be afraid to modify the goal as needed as you live your life.

Fourth, whether we set goals or not, we *will* grow older and time will still march on. Without purpose or goals, our lives will unfold in whatever manner life chooses for us. Our personal outcomes will be unknown to us until they actually happen, often becoming a grave disappointment to us because our fate has been controlled by everything and everyone but ourselves – and we never realized it!

If we don't set goals, we may (or may not) consider ourselves a failure at the end of our lives – but we'll never know for sure until it's too late. Also, a feeling of helplessness sets in during our lives if we falsely believe we are not in control of our own destiny. This belief may be reinforced by the fact that "bad things" keep happening to us, as we drift on a sea of uncertainty, never knowing where we're headed, or even if we're on the right track. If we have no goals, we have no idea what's wrong or what can be corrected. So, we blame outside forces for our problems and don't attempt to correct them ourselves because, "What's the use? They're beyond my control!"

What a terrible waste! How depressing it is to live a life over which we feel we have no control. We must take control of our own destinies by setting goals and then seriously attempting to achieve them.

This is an important distinction. Setting goals without seriously attempting to achieve them (for fear of failing or any other reason) is a useless effort. We may as well not set goals because the end result will be even worse than not setting any goals at all. If we set goals and then don't make a serious effort at achieving them, that's when the real feeling of failure sets in.

A Dangerous Mindset

This sets up the dangerous mindset that justifies not setting goals in the first place. After all, ignorance is bliss, isn't it? If we don't set goals, how can we fail? We'll never realize (or be forced to admit) we've failed to be all we can be if we never acknowledge what we truly desire to achieve in the first place.

In addition, if we do actually happen to achieve something good, we can revel in the joy of what "happened to us" without the consequences of having to face failure if we don't achieve a *specific* goal.

The problem with this kind of thinking is that achieving good things in life is rare if we don't strive for them. Without a plan, we usually don't arrive where we want to be. Even if we do get there, we often don't recognize that we've reached "that place", resulting in vague feelings of dissatisfaction with our lives without knowing why we feel that way.

How many times have we heard of people who reach the end of their lives filled with regret for not having attempted to achieve their dreams? Or see people who seem to "have it all" and are *still* unhappy with what they've got because they don't recognize all the good thing(s) they do have? We see and hear about them all the time. Some of us need only look in the mirror.

This is because, deep in the back of our minds, we all have goals, whether we admit them (to ourselves or others) or not. Feelings of dissatisfaction and discomfort are often related to the fact that, even if we don't consciously acknowledge our dreams and goals, they still exist and don't want to be denied. When they are denied, we feel dissatisfaction and discomfort. Conversely, when they are actually reached, we deny ourselves the reward and self-satisfaction of celebrating an accomplished goal by denying it existed the first place!

We must start taking responsibility for our own success. We must overcome our fear of failure, make a plan and begin our journey. Without taking that first step, we are doomed to fail – either by actually failing to reach our potential, or failing to recognize it once we have reached it.

Overview

Myths to bust:

Myth #1:

If I try to reach a goal and don't make it, I've wasted all that time in between!

Myth #2:

If I don't set goals, I don't fail.

Myth #3:

If I change a goal I have set, that means I've failed, so I can't change my goals – once set, they are carved in stone.

Myth #4:

Bad things just happen to us – that's the destiny of some people. No one can change that.

Myth #5:

Life will somehow wait for me to get my act together – or will just work out OK – whether I set goals or not.

What myths do I buy into?

How can I bust them?

Most common excuses we use to justify our fears and inactivity:

- I'm not afraid – I just don't want to do that
- I don't need to set goals – things are just fine the way they are
- Goal-setting doesn't work; all it does is waste time, and I don't have time to waste

My "favorite" excuses used to justify my fears and inactivity:

Key concepts

Tips to overcome fear and take action:

1. Realize that time marches on, whether or not you set goals, so you may as well start striving for something you can control.

2. If you have never done formal goal-setting before, set a small goal to start with. Make it easily attainable, outline the steps necessary to reach it, and then celebrate when you accomplish the goal.

3. Once you've accomplished one goal, you're ready to set another – or a string of goals to accomplish a larger dream.

Chapter Four

What A Coincidence!

a.k.a. There Is A Reason

I no longer believe in coincidence. I used to… but no longer. Things happen for a reason. I firmly believe that. When we try to push too hard for something to happen, it may be that it simply was not meant to be. This statement's not meant to provide us with a cop-out that enables us to fail and blame fate (or other people) for our failures. It's to make us realize that we're not always supposed to get everything that we try for, in the manner that we try it, or in the timeframe we expect it.

However, the situation won't be resolved unless you take action – either by doing it yourself, or by asking for help from others.

Don't be afraid to ask for help

Don't be too proud or cynical to ask for help. Don't think that just because it's not easy, no one will help you. You would be surprised at how many people will come to the aid of someone with a strong will and commitment to succeed and change.

Often help comes in the form of a message from a friend, or a stranger destined to become a friend. Just when you think you're at your lowest point, something (or someone) can come along and "rescue" you if you recognize the gift and accept it. If you don't recognize the seemingly "coincidental" things that happen to you, these gifts could pass you by.

Here are some of the "coincidences" that have occurred in my life:

- On the day after my business partnership unexpectedly ended, one of my best friends called and told me another friend had died, unexpectedly and at a very early age, of a massive heart attack. As depressed as I was over my failed partnership, this news made me realize that while my problem was very upsetting, at least I was still here to enjoy the rest of my life – so my problem wasn't so big, after all.
- When I sold real estate in RI, I met and began working with an attorney with whom I was to close several transactions. On the day of one of my closings, I experienced a sudden serious medical problem. On the way to see my doctor, my pager rang at the exact moment when I was passing this attorney's office. It was the attorney, calling me about the closing later that day. I told my assistant (who was driving me to the doctor's office, since I couldn't drive) to pull into his office so I could see what he needed. When I hobbled into his office, he asked what was wrong and upon hearing I was in medical trouble, made a call to one of his best friends – who just happened to be one of the best surgeons in the state. *Coincidentally*, it turned out that I did need a surgeon, and could have had serious residual problems had I not had someone of his caliber to operate on me.
- At one point, my husband and I wanted to sell our home in Lincoln, RI and buy a condominium in Bristol, RI. We put $20,000 down on the condo, then couldn't sell the house.

> Finally, we decided to take the house off the market and get our condominium deposit back. We got our money back just two weeks before the big S&L crash occurred. In our state, the credit union used by the builder to hold our deposit was one of the worst hit, causing many people to either lose their money, or to have to wait up to five years to get it back. We had gotten our money out just in time! This event also helped create a serious recession in RI, causing the condominium we *would have* bought (if we'd been able to sell our home) to **decrease** in value by $100,000 over the next 5 years!! It eventually came back 5 years later, but we were saved from this debacle by the mere fact that we couldn't get what we wanted in the first place.

There are many more stories like this in my own life. I'm sure you have many of your own. My life has taken so many twists and turns, all seemingly unrelated and/or coincidental. But when I really look, I see many situations that had been "set up" by others, and I think to myself, "Wow! If *that* hadn't happened, I never would have been here to do this . . ." and wonder where I would have ended up.

Often I have looked back at what seemed at the time to be "bad" situations, only to see that everything turned out much better in the end because that "bad" thing had occurred!

There's an old saying that I firmly believe, that "When God closes a door, He opens a window." I have seen this happen countless times in my life. In many instances, the open window stands obviously before me, showing me what I have to do. In others, the answer came later, in hindsight, as I see where my life could have led if the tragedy (or what I perceived as a tragedy at the time) had not occurred to spur me on to something new. And in other instances, I am still waiting for the answer to come to me, for the window to open, so that I can make some rhyme or reason out of what happened, and why. I may never find the answers in this life, as to why some of these events occurred, but I am certain there is a reason... I must simply be patient enough to wait for that explanation to come to me in its own time.

Overview

Myths to bust:

Myth #1:

Things don't "happen for a reason" – they just happen!

Myth #2:

People will not be able to (or want to) help me – especially if I need a lot of ongoing help.

Myth #3:

If I can't do it on my own, it's not worth doing it all. I don't need any help!

What myths do I buy into?

____

____

How can I bust them?

____

____

Most common excuses we use to justify our fears and inactivity:

- No one will help me, so why bother asking?
- No one would help me – that's why I failed. I'll never try that again!
- It just isn't/wasn't meant to be, so forget about it. I give up!
- I don't really believe I can do it, so I don't want to tell anyone else I'm trying to do it!
- If it happens great; if not – oh, well!

My "favorite" excuses used to justify my fears and inactivity:

Tips to overcome fear and take action:

1. Write down occurrences of strange "coincidences" as they happen. Look back on them periodically to see if they've actually turned into something different (or better) than you thought they originally were – or if they sparked other positive events in your life. As you recognize more and more of these, it will give you confidence to trust what happens and react positively, rather than becoming depressed and immobilized over seemingly negative events.

2. Determine what you want to do – think it through and write down the steps that need to be accomplished. When you think a project through, you're much more likely to act on it, than if you just say you want to do it without having any idea on earth how to go about doing it!

3. Determine who you may need to help you. Then ask that person for help! Get over your fear that they'll say, "No." Even if they do, you'll be no worse off than before you asked!

4. Tell other people about your dreams. Even if you don't need or receive their help, you can still use their encouragement.

Chapter Five

How Did That Happen?

a.k.a. The Role of Cause & Effect

Everything happens for a reason. Whether we can immediately see what caused the event is irrelevant. Sometimes the reasons are within our control; sometimes they are beyond it. No matter what the reason, unless we deliberately search for the causes and effects of our actions and circumstances, we will continue to believe that events just "happen" to us, rather than being in our control. This results in a feeling of helplessness, causing us to give up hope of ever achieving our dreams. Why not? Since it's all just "random chance", why bother trying to make anything turn out the way we want it to?

It's important to look behind the events that occur in our lives to see what prior actions may have caused them, since they don't just "happen" all by themselves. By doing so, we can not only prevent a negative effect from recurring, but duplicate a positive effect.

For example, in the world of sales, a lack of appropriate prospecting for a period of as short as 30 days could cause a resultant shortage in personal income in as little as 90 days. If you're in a sales business and see a slump in your income, look back about 90 days to the business-building activities you did (or didn't do) at that time; you will usually see a direct correlation between a drop in business-building activity and a drop in business and income. The length of the gap (which usually corresponds to the average length of the sales cycle) may vary from industry to industry, but the correlation is undeniable.

The unfortunate part of this scenario is that we don't immediately see how that temporary drop in activity will affect us later, so we believe (or hope) the unfortunate result will not happen. Only experience – ours or that of others – will demonstrate it. Learning from the experience of others helps us avoid experiencing this pain ourselves. If we've learned it personally, it can be a hard lesson, but hopefully one that won't need to be repeated.

This scenario bears itself out in thousands of other daily personal and professional situations. There is always a cause and effect, always an action and a reaction. The key is determining which specific actions cause which reactions, and eliminating those that cause negative reactions while increasing those that cause positive ones.

The link between cause and effect

Let's look at an absurdly simple, yet accurate, example of cause and effect. When we have an itch, we scratch it automatically, without thinking . . . why? Because it's so annoying and insistent that we must do something about it – NOW! We don't sit around and complain about how much our back itches, or how much we'd like the itch to magically disappear. We do something about it – and it works! We scratch the itch and it goes away.

Why will we scratch an itch, yet not take care of other things we really want to do in life?

The first reason is that scratching an itch is EASY! We do something about the itch because it's easy for us to reach around and scratch it. If it's in a place that's hard to reach, we ask someone else to do it for us. They do it because (you guessed it!)... it's easy. Most people will take action if it's quick and easy to do.

This brings us to the second reason why most people will take action in certain circumstances: they can see instant results from their efforts. In the case of scratching an itch, cause and effect are easy to see; the link is obvious since the effect occurs immediately after the action is taken.

However, other cause-and-effect relationships in life are not so simple to relate to each other. Things don't always happen instantly to demonstrate the link between one action (or an entire group of actions) and the effect caused by that action, or lack thereof. Significant delays often occur between cause and effect, obscuring the true cause of the effect.

In addition, if the result is too long in coming or too difficult to accomplish, many give up long before *enough* action has been taken to see any results. Even if they claim to really want to accomplish something, many people will not exercise the patience and commitment to stick with all the steps necessary to complete the task, especially if the results take longer than expected.

If the result is too long in coming or too difficult to accomplish, many give up long before *enough* action has been taken to see any results.

Unfortunately, when something bothers us, it's not always easy or quick to eliminate or change it. However, it *is* easy just to sit back and complain, wasting hours, days, months and years of our lives wishing it weren't so, or blaming others for our situation. Soon, we're looking back on a life lost wishing for things that never had a chance to occur because we didn't have the strength or commitment to make them happen. Rather than just complaining about our circumstances, we must recognize that action, not complaints, cause the changes we desire.

Key Principles for Guiding Cause and Effect

1. Stop looking for instant gratification

We hear the term "instant gratification" bantered around a lot. It's an important term! We've become an impatient society, always looking for the instant solution or "quick fix", as if a solution that comes quickly and without effort is the answer to all our problems – or even reasonable to expect!

> **Action, not complaints, cause the changes we desire.**

However, this term clearly illustrates why we will scratch that itch, but will not follow through on other things. A scratched itch instantly disappears! Most of our other accomplishments are not so quick in coming. When something doesn't happen instantly, human nature is such that most of us are easily de-motivated, abandoning the actions we've planned because we can't see the light at the end of the tunnel. Gratification doesn't come soon enough for us, and we don't have the patience to wait for it to come, or even to wait until we can *see* it coming.

2. Stop creating unreasonable expectations

When we create unreasonable expectations for ourselves, we are doomed to fail, simply because true success is not often gained that easily. Many of our problems stem from the fact that we don't give ourselves a fair chance to achieve our goals, nor do we allot an appropriate timeframe or budget for them. When we expect things to fall into place instantly – and then they don't – we experience doubt in our own abilities, fear that it won't happen, and frustration with our setbacks, causing us to give up prematurely when things don't go our way.

This applies not only to our expectations of ourselves, but our expectations of others, as well. We must allow each other to be human and stop putting that kind of pressure on ourselves and others. Many more problems are caused by the unrealistic expectations of other people in our lives. This is where we must become stronger, and not allow others to place unrealistic expectations on us.

3. Stop and think before you act – make a plan

Envisioning the possible consequences (positive or negative) of your actions before you act is much more easily said than done. It is, however, the key to preventing many undesirable consequences of acting too quickly.

Thinking things through (and actually writing them down) will help you accomplish several things:

- It allows you to itemize all (or most) of the steps necessary to accomplish your goals.
- It allows you to put those steps in logical order.
- It causes you to think of possible scenarios that could result from the contemplated action and allow you to capitalize on the positive while minimizing or eliminating the negative.
- You can create backup plans, just in case an undesirable event occurs, allowing you to get back on track much more quickly than if you try to think while in the middle of a crisis.
- It also allows you to stop yourself before performing an action that may cause unnecessary harm.

4. Take Action – NOW!

This is the phase in which we implement our plan. Once we've had time to think things through and write them down, we've probably regained at least some of our lost confidence, even when we've already made mistakes that have damaged it.

Once we have a plan, we can take action. Most of us stop at the point of action because we're unsure what to do, or we allow ourselves to continue to procrastinate because there are no deadlines – after all, "there's always tomorrow!"

Beginning to implement the plan and experiencing success with the first steps supplies us with added courage and encouragement to go on and accomplish further steps.

5. Allow yourself to make, and learn from, mistakes

This also fits into the category of unreasonable expectations. It's amazing how many times we try new things, then beat ourselves up when we aren't perfect on the very first try!

We must admit, right from the start, that we probably won't execute every step along the way perfectly. By giving ourselves permission to be imperfect, we can plan for mistakes, have resources ready to correct them if they occur, and give ourselves permission to try again without further unreasonable expectations getting in the way.

6. Don't beat yourself up if it doesn't happen overnight

One of the consequences of failure to achieve a goal is self-punishment. We beat ourselves up for not knowing the unknowable. Often, we follow the punishment phase with wallowing in self-pity and regret.

Regret gets us nowhere. By focusing on how badly we feel about not achieving success, we delay success even longer. We cannot fix the problem and try again if we stagnate at the stage of punishment and regret for what's gone wrong.

We must quickly figure out what went wrong, learn how to correct the situation and get on with trying again! The only way I know to move forward is to stop holding myself back and get going. Just because something hasn't succeeded yet doesn't mean it won't succeed at all.

7. Don't Measure Yourself Against Others, Especially If They Are Exceptions To The Rule

We must learn patience, and allow success to come in due time. Many of us quit just before we would have been successful because we're so busy comparing ourselves to "the other guy" who was successful quickly. We assume that if our own success doesn't come as quickly, it won't come at all – and we give up!

After my first year in real estate, but before I had succeeded myself, I heard stories of other people who had made over $100,000, or closed 75 transactions *in their first year*, causing me to wonder why I hadn't been able to do as well in my first year of sales. I had come home almost nightly during that first year (and even into the second) and told my husband, "Honey, I don't think I'm going to make it. I don't think I can do this!" But something wouldn't let me quit and finally, I did make it! If I had quit before giving myself an adequate chance to rectify all the issues that arose, I would never have experienced the big success that came later.

What I didn't realize was that those people's goals and priorities, personalities, experiences, and markets ALL played a role in their early successes. In addition, I didn't realize that many were exceptions to the rule, since these are the ones that receive the most publicity. It doesn't usually happen that way.

If we try to measure ourselves against these exceptions to the rule, we're guaranteed to fail. We must not give in to feelings of inadequacy, fear and jealousy in order to achieve something someone else achieved, even when those expectations are unrealistic.

8. Be persistent – don't quit!

To repeat, our society is much too focused on instant gratification. It isn't reasonable; it isn't possible. This attitude will destroy us if we continue to expect it. It may take weeks, months or years for success, depending on our ultimate goals. It may take several tries to get one step in the action plan right so we can progress to the next step.

However, if we persist and make progress every day, learn from every experience and commit to practicing and getting better with each new obstacle, success will happen! The only way we stop progressing forward is if we fail to persist in making progress. If we don't quit, we won't lose!

Avoiding a chain-reaction of depressive behavior

It would be very easy to allow ourselves to wallow in self-pity instead of pulling ourselves out of our depression and changing the course of negative events. Obviously, I'm not talking about situations that would qualify as clinical depression, which may necessitate professional help to work through the depression. I'm referring to normal situations we all experience where we allow one "failure" to start a chain-reaction that could cause other, unnecessary, failures if we don't catch it quickly and reverse the cycle.

There are several phases of this process, defined as follows:

Phase I: Recognition and acknowledgement of the problem

Before we can correct any situation, we must first recognize and acknowledge that a problem exists, take responsibility for our part in it, and recognize that its solution is within our control.

It is at this point that we must stop blaming others for our problems or circumstances, stop trying to force society – and everyone in it – to treat us "fairly" and begin to understand that success is solely in our hands.

Life is not always fair. Many people fight human nature and waste their lives trying to change the way things are. Successful people accept human nature and find the best way to succeed despite parameters beyond their control by working effectively with those within their control.

Once, when I was selling real estate, this lesson was taught to me by an attorney who, when I railed against "the unfair way the laws worked", said to me, "Sandy, I don't make the laws. I agree with you – they're not fair and what's happening now is not right. However, we can continue to debate its unfairness, or we can identify what we can do to fix the problem and get going on the solution." This was great advice – and I've never forgotten it.

Once we stop railing against what's unfair, and start working on ways to deal with it, we're on the road to success.

Phase II: Separation and compartmentalization

This also means that, once we discover an area that needs correction, we must not allow any resultant depression to spill over into multiple areas. Unfortunately, if depression occurs as a result of a single problem (or set of problems), we often blur the true reason for the depression and begin doubting our abilities in other areas. Maybe a family situation is not going well. This has nothing to do with our career, and yet we may begin to doubt our ability to "do anything right" – even going so far as to verbalize statements to that effect, either silently or out loud.

We must stop this destructive kind of self-talk and realize that temporary setbacks in one area do not completely undermine our ability to be successful in other areas. By putting different areas of our lives and success into different "compartments", separating themselves from each other, we can treat success and failure in each area objectively enough to correct a problem in one area without sabotaging success in another.

> **Compartmentalization allows us to treat success and failure in each area objectively enough to correct a problem in one area without sabotaging success in another.**

It is crucial to continue to truly believe in ourselves and our abilities in order to get through these times. Believing in ourselves and our abilities allows us to get past the temporary feelings of unworthiness and truly believe that we are capable – and worthy – of success. This belief is what enables us to separate the successful areas of our lives from those that still need work, and to go on to the next phase of our journey toward determining and implementing a solution.

Phase III: Recognition of our behavior patterns

Before we can separate our feelings, we must first recognize what we do when we become depressed. Do we follow certain patterns? Do we allow that depression to spill over into other situations? Do we do things that actually cause us to become more depressed, such as isolating ourselves, listening to sad music, or indulging in excessive behaviors such as eating or sleeping?

Until we recognize what we do when we're depressed, we will never be able to put a stop to it and take action that will help pull us out of the depression. In Chapter Seven, we'll take a closer look at the behavior patterns we follow when we're depressed, so we can reverse this cycle.

Phase IV: Regain and Maintain Belief in Yourself

One way to stop negative behaviors when things go wrong and prevent spillover into other areas of our lives is to focus on past accomplishments. Even though it may be difficult to recall these events when we're depressed, it's a great way to regain faith in ourselves. There are many ways to overcome this difficulty. We can call loved ones who can help us focus on our good qualities and past achievements.

Another helpful action is to call a past client with whom we've had successful dealings. Talking with them will reinforce the fact that we have been successful at helping others achieve their goals.

A third option is to think back on our own past successes and begin making a plan to create other successes using a proven formula.

Whatever it takes, we must regain faith in our ability to succeed – and then strive to maintain that faith throughout the difficult situation. Doing this will allow us to make it through to the other side, where we will begin to see progress once more toward our goals.

Phase V: Determination and Implementation of a Solution

This is the phase in which we've been able to separate our feelings of self-doubt and "failure", and focus on a solution to the problem at hand. We may have needed time in a previous phase to grieve over the situation that initially caused the stress, but once the grieving period is over, it's time to decide what to do in order to go on.

We must think things through, ponder the situation for a while. We may want to discuss it with a trusted family member or colleague. Then we can write out planned actions, including deadlines and budgets, if necessary. Once we've decided on a course of action, it's time to implement it and get back on track.

Myths to bust:

Overview

Myth #1:

Big success is all luck anyway, so nothing I do will change anything. You just have to be in the right place, at the right time and just get lucky!

Myth #2:

I can't see any adverse effect of my actions right now, so they probably won't hurt me later.

Myth #3:

If success doesn't come quickly, it's not worth it.

Myth #4:

If I don't achieve success as quickly as someone else, I must not be as capable as that person.

What myths do I buy into?

___

___

How can I bust them?

___

___

Most common excuses we use to justify our fears and inactivity:

- I knew this would never work for me!
- I'm just not that lucky!
- Nothing ever goes right for me.
- My whole life is a failure, so why bother?
- I can't seem to do anything right.

My "favorite" excuses used to justify my fears and inactivity:

Tips to overcome fear and take action:

1. Figure out which actions cause negative effects and which cause positive ones, and work on eliminating the wrong ones while focusing on the right ones.
2. Look at your goals and compare your actions to their direct effect on accomplishment of those goals. If an action moves you further away from your goal, stop doing it. If an action moves you closer to your goal, start doing more of it.
3. Look at your positive and negative actons in order to analyze how they affect you.
   a. What triggers them – negative or positive events?
   b. How do you feel when you're doing them – guilty, confused and angry or positive, healthy and happy?
   c. Are others whom you love, respect and trust telling you to stop doing them – or to continue doing them?

NOTE: Are a combination of the above factors occurring in your life? For example, are those you love telling you to stop doing an action AND you feel terrible while you're doing it AND it's not getting you any closer to your goal?

This is an important point because sometimes others will tell you not to do something, but you have faith it will lead you in the right direction AND you feel good when you do it. Even if you're making mistakes, if the mistakes are helping you accomplish a new task AND it's steering you in the direction of your dreams, don't let other people's fear and uncertainty stop you from accomplishing a difficult or long-term dream in which you have faith, but they don't.

Continued

4. Avoid a chain-reaction of depressive behavior
   a. Phase I: Recognize and acknowledge the problem
   b. Phase II: Separate and compartmentalize problem areas
   c. Phase III: Recognize your behavior patterns
   d. Phase IV: Regain and maintain belief in yourself
   e. Phase V: Determine and Implement a Solution

Key Principles for Guiding Cause and Effect:

1. Stop looking for instant gratification! Give any positive action enough time to see its beneficial effects before giving up on it.
2. Stop creating unreasonable expectations.
3. Stop and think before you act – make a plan.

NOTE: Don't wait for it to be PERFECT!! IT never will be. But at least give yourself a fighting chance by preparing for all obvious and foreseeable circumstances.

4. Take action – NOW!
5. Allow yourself to make, and learn from, mistakes.
6. Don't beat yourself up if it doesn't happen overnight.
7. Don't measure yourself against others, especially if they are exceptions to the rule.
8. Be persistent – don't quit!

Chapter Six

Life Stinks! (Or Does It?)

a.k.a. How Do We View Tragedy?

What is *tragedy*, anyway? Many of us confuse daily, normal, to-be-expected setbacks with true tragedy. What we often call tragedy is usually not the life-altering event intended by this word. According to the dictionary, the word *tragedy* has many meanings. One definition offered is our normal view of this word: *a very sad or tragic event or events; a disaster.* However, it is interesting to note that this is actually the *sixth* and final definition given for the word. The first definition is as follows: *a serious play typically dealing with the problems of a central character, leading to an unhappy or disastrous ending brought on, as in ancient drama, by fate and a tragic flaw in this character, or in modern drama, usually by moral weakness, psychological maladjustment or social pressures.*

Whew! That is one complex definition. The most significant portion of the definition deals with the fact that no matter how many terrible things happen during a play, it cannot be classified as a tragedy until it culminates in an unhappy or disastrous ending. Also, an important point not to be missed is that the ending is brought on by the character himself, due to a combination of fate and tragic flaws in the character's psychological make-up.

In ancient drama, the tragic outcome was determined by fate and helped along by a tragic personality that prevented the character from coping with uncontrollable events caused by an unseen hand. However, in our more educated and enlightened society, we see the shift in modern drama as we recognize that most tragedies are not caused by external forces (fate), but by our own attitudes and actions, as well as our reactions to the events that occur in our lives.

These concepts are at work in our everyday lives.

When events unfold, whether small or all-encompassing, true tragedy does not (and cannot) occur until a story *ends* in disaster or unhappiness.

True tragedy does not (and cannot) occur until a story ends in disaster or unhappiness.

We all create the stories of our lives as we live them. Just as we see examples of people who can take a seemingly unrecoverable disaster and triumph in spite of it, we all know people who can take the smallest event and blow it so out of proportion that they create a tragedy where none should exist.

Crucial contrast

Negative events are crucial in our lives if we are to ever appreciate the positive ones. If we never had rainy days, how could we appreciate the beauty of the sun sparkling off the water in the ocean? Without clouds, could we see cloud shadows dance across a meadow? If the weather were never hot and muggy, we'd never fully appreciate the refreshing sensation of cooling off by jumping into a lake or pool, or by standing in the stream of a fire hydrant's cold water.

There's an old joke that goes like this: "Why are you banging your head against the wall?" Answer: "Because it feels so good when I stop!"

Without the contrast of pain and pleasure, we could never fully appreciate the good things that occur in life. The problem lies in the fact that, while negative events are just as essential as positive ones, we must not allow them to turn into tragedies that overshadow and destroy our lives and the lives of everyone around us.

As we all know, it is not what happens to us that determines the course of our lives, but how we react to positive and negative events as they occur.

Overcoming my biggest personal obstacle

I once read about a woman named Danielle Kennedy, who grew up believing she had inherited from her mother a medical problem that would prevent her from having children of her own. All her life, she was prepared for this eventuality. However, she married and conceived a child on her honeymoon, freeing her from the inner constraints she had put on herself anticipating problems that hadn't happened yet (and, in fact, would never happen).

I had just the opposite problem. Although my mother did have some problems having children, I never thought that I would have a problem. So, when faced with the fact that I would not be able to have children, I was taken completely by surprise. My husband and I tried everything we knew (and could afford) for almost 10 years; nothing worked.

We then tried adoption, but in the early 1980's it was not as easy to adopt as it has become today. We were told by the largest adoption agency in Providence, RI that because our home wasn't "childless" (my husband's two children lived with us), they wouldn't place a child in our home. Children from their agency were only placed in "childless" homes. We tried to explain that *I* was childless, but that didn't matter. Apparently, they felt that if I threw my husband's children out into the street, I would be much better "motherhood material".

We couldn't afford the $10,000 for private domestic adoption, so that avenue was closed to us. In addition, due to innumerable and severely restrictive country rules, international adoption was not an option, either.

When confronted with a crisis of this magnitude, you begin to rethink a lot of things. I do firmly believe there is a reason for everything that happens to us. However, during my struggle to conceive a child, it was hard to keep this in mind.

For a while, it was difficult even to watch TV, since every commercial and television show seemed to focus on babies and people having them. I also remember one news story that will stay with me forever. At the height of my frustration and despair, a story was published in the local newspaper about an infant's body that had been found in a plastic bag in a trashcan. Somewhere, a mother had discarded her own child like she would kitchen trash, while I desperately wanted a child and couldn't have one!

I raged at myself, my husband, the world and God himself that He would deny me a child, yet allow someone like that to have one, only to callously destroy it. It seemed inconceivable, yet it was true. Why these things happen, no one knows.

It took a while, but I finally came to accept the fact that I wasn't meant to have children of my own. It wasn't easy. I can talk about it now only because so much time has passed and I have grown stronger with the healing that only time can bring.

However, at that crucial point in my life, there were two roads I could have taken: one was to accept and go on, and be the best stepmother I could be to my husband's children; the other was to refuse to accept the situation and become bitter and angry with the world, destroying my life and my marriage and negatively impacting several other lives in the process. I chose to accept and go on.

While the magnitude of this choice is not typical of those all of us face every day, we all do face daily choices that positively or negatively impact our lives. Without a driving commitment to overcome any obstacle in our way, expected or not, we will fail to achieve all that is possible in life.

Overcoming Enormous Tragedy

When we see someone who has faced an enormous tragedy, we think to ourselves, "Wow. I could never be that strong. I don't know how he or she did that." We simply can't relate to something that overwhelming in our own lives because we haven't had the necessity or opportunity to do so.

Right! What an opportunity! Wouldn't we all wish to have a terrible tragedy befall us, so we'd have an *opportunity* to deal with it? Of course not. I'm not saying this is something we would, or should, wish for. What I am saying is that when tragedies befall us, we must look at the event as a turning point in our lives. We can either choose to let the event destroy our lives – creating a true tragedy – or we can decide that we're strong enough to overcome it.

The problem is that most of us don't believe we could be strong enough to do so. What's interesting is that many people who thrive after overwhelming tragedy previously believed they never would have been strong enough to survive something of that magnitude, either. So it is possible…

Many people who truly thrive after overwhelming tragedy previously believed they never would have been strong enough to survive something of that magnitude.

In order to avoid tragedy and achieve happiness and success, we must get through the obstacles and find our way to the other side. But how do we get through obstacles and depression? One way is to recognize what we do when we're depressed and prevent our depression from sabotaging our efforts at success.

In the next chapter, we'll take a hard look at exactly what we customarily do that either lifts or fosters depression.

Overview

Myths to bust:

Myth #1:

A tragedy occurs at the outset of a big problem; therefore, any big problem can be considered a true tragedy, and there's not much we can do about it.

Myth #2:

People who overcome true adversity have an inner pool of resources that the average person doesn't have.

Myth #3:

Most people are not strong enough to handle true adversity. Very few people can do this – and I'm not one of them.

What myths do I buy into?

____

____

How can I bust them?

____

____

Most common excuses we use to justify our fears and inactivity:

- This is the worst thing that could have ever happened! It shouldn't have happened! It's not fair!
- I'll never recover from this.
- I'll never be able to get over this!
- I'm not strong enough. I can't handle that!
- No one should be required to handle that! No one *could* handle that!
- I'm too embarrassed to go back and admit I made a mistake (or ask forgiveness, or ask for help)

My "favorite" excuses used to justify my fears and inactivity:

Tips to overcome fear and take action:

1. Look at each situation that occurs and objectively determine its true impact.

2. Remember that true tragedy does not occur unless you give up trying to improve your situation. Determine how you can get out of the situation quickly, before it *becomes* a tragedy.

3. No matter how severe your situation, examine and use what you can learn from the lessons demonstrated by others who have faced true adversity and triumphed.

4. Call someone who has faced adversity and triumphed and ask for advice, assistance, moral support. People are very willing to offer help to those courageous enough to ask for it.

Chapter Seven

I Don't Feel Like It!

a.k.a. What Do We Do When We're Depressed?

What do we do when we're sad, or when something bad happens? Unfortunately, human nature too easily allows us to do all the wrong things when we need to avoid falling into depression, or need to climb out of one quickly. We need to break the negative cycle that begins at these times!

For example, when I'm feeling depressed, I often catch myself putting on sad, mournful music to match my mood, listening to tales of woe that break my heart and leave me feeling hopeless! This is probably one of the *worst* things I could do when I'm already sad, lonely or depressed; yet, that's my first instinct.

Think back to a time when you have heard a sad song. Didn't you think to yourself, "Oh, yeah. I know that feeling. I can identify with that." I know I have. This is exactly why sad music is so popular. Those mournful chords and heartbreaking lyrics are specifically *designed* to move us emotionally. That's why they are so powerful. The lyrics also touch a chord in us because we can all strongly identify with the singer and the situation being described through their words. It's very easy to allow those sad lyrics and the emotions conjured up by the music to drag us further down, allowing us to immerse ourselves in the tragedy that has befallen someone else, taking on more and more depression in the process – until we feel we can never break free.

Don't get me wrong; mellow music is not something to be avoided at all cost. When we're in a strong, upbeat frame of mind, we can separate ourselves from the singer and the song, enjoy the beautiful melodies and appreciate the temporary nature of the tragedy unfolding in the lyrics. However, when we're in a vulnerable state of mind, those effects can be devastating. Instead of merely emotionally moving us, they enable depression to take on a life of its own.

When we're in a vulnerable state of mind, the effects of sad music can be devastating.

If I'm really depressed, it takes all my willpower to turn off that type of music and either listen to nothing, or listen to more upbeat music. If you have the same reaction, you must fight the urge to drag yourself deeper into depression through sad music. Force yourself to listen to more upbeat music when you get that depressed feeling, to help lift yourself out of it.

While some people listen to music, others do different activities when they're depressed, including isolating themselves, drinking too much, eating too much (or too little), and other negative responses.

When we find ourselves doing something negative, or wasting time complaining about something rather than doing something constructive, we must perform a positive action to counteract it. We may need to change or fix a particular situation. If the situation is one that we can't fix or control, we must let it go and do something positive that will give us a reasonable expectation of success in another area.

For example, a real estate saleswoman I once knew constantly complained about the extended waiting time from contract to closing when selling homes. In addition, she had an unreasonable fear of being "screwed" out of a commission.

Once she realized the negative energy she was expending constantly complaining and worrying about circumstances beyond her control, instead of complaining to anyone who would listen, she decided that as soon as she caught herself voicing complaints about a situation (or even just thinking and obsessing about it *yet again*), she would make a prospecting phone call to try to drum up new business.

Allow fear and frustration to become a trigger for positive action.

This was a positive action (with a reasonable expectation of success) that counteracted the negative, time-consuming activity of complaining about something that couldn't be changed. By doing this, she allowed her fear and frustration with a situation to become a trigger for positive action, rather than sitting back and complaining about how lousy things were. It worked! By making those calls, she got more business, very effectively lifting her frustration and depression!

The following is a very short list of typical things we do when we become depressed, as well as some suggestions to counteract depression. I realize these suggestions may not be easy to do. (Of course, all of them require that we recognize when we're performing these activities due to depression.)

It takes a lot of willpower to break bad habits, and we may not do them perfectly every time. However, until we recognize dangerous or destructive behavior patterns and begin to change them, we will never eliminate or overcome their effects.

Recognizing and counteracting behaviors that further depression

Behavior:	**Solution:**
Isolate ourselves from our friends and families	Call a close friend or family member, or visit or meet them. If you're feeling down about business, call a satisfied past client who can bolster your confidence in your abilities, services and/or products.
Escape into the fantasyland of books, movies, etc.	Read uplifting or motivational books, listen to motivational CD's and tapes that will spur you to action of your own, rather than ones that fuel fear and depression.
Listen to sad music	Create a tape or CD of upbeat music, and play it whenever you need to. When you feel the urge to play sad music due to depression, play the upbeat tape or CD.
Sleep too much	Exercise – this will usually give you more energy.

Sleep too little	Just before going to bed, meditate; try progressive relaxation techniques; try aroma therapy; read a book in bed.
Over-eat	Join a gym or weight management plan; hire a personal trainer to come to your home or meet you at the gym; call a friend when you feel like snacking; snack on healthy foods; don't keep junk food in the house to tempt you; enlist the help of your family and friends.
Under-eat	Force yourself to eat or drink something healthy several times a day, even if it's just a little bit at a time. If the problem is severe enough, you may need professional help to overcome this problem.
Drink too much	If this is a minor problem, do something else when you find yourself reaching for another glass of wine, beer or hard liquor. (see below: take a break). If this is a serious problem, you may need professional assistance to change this behavior.

Take drugs	Obviously, if this is an ongoing problem, you will likely need professional assistance to change this behavior.
Spend money	Avoid the mall, online stores, etc. Take a short break: go for a walk, exercise, clean the house, play a computer game. (As silly as it may sound, I love taking a short break to play Solitaire or Free Cell; when I win, I feel as though I've accomplished at least ONE thing!)
Seek out the wrong people and activities	Before making that call, or going to the wrong "hang-out", wait 5 minutes and play out in your mind what will probably happen if you go there. If it really is the wrong thing to do, the outcome will be negative. If it's negative, don't do it. Do something positive instead (see above: take a short break).

Wallow in our pain, anger or fear, perpetuating it and turning it into something bigger than it originally was	Stop reliving the negative experience in your mind. When you find yourself thinking about it, get up and do something to take your mind off it.
Worry (often needlessly) about things getting worse, instead of focusing on fixing the problem and making things better	Analyze the situation. Ask yourself: What's the worst thing that could happen? Usually, it's not as bad as what you're imagining before objectively analyzing the situation. If you (or someone else) are not going to die, it's probably not that bad! It may end up being embarrassing, but no one has ever died of embarrassment.
Blame others for our troubles	Stop blaming anyone or anything and make a plan of action to change things. Look ahead, not back.

As you can see, a great solution to many of these behaviors is to take a short break to stop the pattern of negative behavior. When you go back to the problem after taking a break and performing any of the above activities (or similar positive activities) in place of destructive ones, your mind will have continued working on the problem in the background, and you may discover a solution that had previously escaped you.

Tips for remaining positive in your outlook on life

Eliminate (or at the very least, reduce) contact with negative people in your life.

How often have we heard (or had to live with) "constant complainers", those people who never see the good in anything, and in fact can often find something bad in situations that 99% of the population would view positively?

I recall a time when my husband and I took a cruise (not usually an inexpensive proposition). Even when you can get a good last-minute deal, as we did, a lot of planning and expense are necessary to make any vacation successful. Thus, a natural assumption would be that anyone who goes through all that effort would intend to *try* to have a good time. Bad assumption...

There were four couples assigned to our dinner table and, except for certain days in port, we were to dine together every night. One of the couples at our table were two very sweet people who somehow managed to find fault with *everything*, from the menu choices to the temperature and taste of the food to the fact that they wanted a window in their cabin and only got a porthole. They complained about the ports, the entertainment and every topic that arose during dinner conversation. My husband and I were seated right beside them and found ourselves dreading dinnertime by the third night – and there were 10 nights on the cruise! This couple managed to ruin their own enjoyment as well as the enjoyment of everyone else at the table with their constant complaining and failure to see the good in any situation.

Do you know people who go through life in this miserable state? Do they ever enjoy anything? Do any of the people in their lives enjoy anything with them? Not likely.

If you have these people in your life (and most of us do at one time or another), eliminate or reduce your contact with them so they don't drag you down with them. Even if this is difficult or impossible, recognizing that their attitudes don't have to affect yours will help you compartmentalize their emotional impact on you. While you're with them, allow them to vent, recognize that this is their pattern, let it roll off your back, and as soon as they're gone do something positive to counteract the impact of their negative energy.

Recognize and eliminate your own negative thoughts and behaviors

If you recognize these behavior patterns in your own actions, start trying to find positive things in life to appreciate, rather than always focusing on the one bad thing that happens on a vacation, or on the holiday, or during dinner at your favorite restaurant…

Do you constantly find yourself saying, "I really liked that meal, but…"? If the statement that follows the "but" is insignificant, let it go! Focus on the first part of the statement, where you can recognize that you really liked the meal – and stop thinking up things to ruin the enjoyment you did experience.

Allow yourself to mourn and/or vent, but don't let it go on too long

Sometimes it's necessary and cathartic to allow yourself to "mourn" a particular event, and even to vent about it. In these cases, don't deny yourself the healing power of these activities.

The problem occurs when we allow them to go on too long, and they pass the point of being therapeutic, crossing over into the area of hindering or delaying our recovery from unfortunate events in our lives.

Find someone you trust, who loves and cares about you, to whom you can honestly talk and vent when necessary. You may even be their "sounding board" when things get tough for them. However, know when it's time to stop. If you can't determine for yourself when it's time to stop doing so, ask them to tell you if they believe it's going on too long, or becoming too severe, for your own good. Listen to them, take their advice and stop!

Keep a "joke file" handy (either printed or electronic), so you can read and view funny materials – cartoons, jokes, cards – when you're feeling down or stressed.

You can keep a file at work and at home, so that whenever you (or someone else around you) needs a lift, you can go to the file and pick an appropriate piece of humor to dispel negative energy.

Jokes and cartoons abound everywhere – from the newspaper to magazines to the Internet to the e-mails you receive. When you find something that strikes your funny bone, copy it to your computer and then print it out for future reference and laughs! You'll be glad you did. It is not a violation of copyright laws to print and/or save these items for your own personal use when you need a laugh – or when a friend needs one. Just don't sell or re-publish them.

Don't lose the wonder and enjoyment (even of very small things) that you possessed when you were a child and were discovering things for the first time.

No matter who tells you something to the contrary, we are never too "cool" or "grown-up" to notice and marvel at incredible things in our world, such as a plane taking off, or puffs of clouds that look like huge cotton balls in the sky, or lightning dancing in and around the clouds during a storm.

We've all become so accustomed to advanced technology that we take things for granted, such as TV, radio, telephone, movies. When microwave ovens first came out, we were scared of them! I remember being in a high school science class discussing the first piece of chicken cooked in something called a "microwave oven". Everyone I knew (students, teachers, and parents alike) marveled at this invention! No one was too "cool" to recognize it for what it was: a brand new appliance that was incredible - and also very scary! Of course, at that time everyone in the class swore that we'd probably get radiation poisoning from it, so we would NEVER eat anything that was cooked in THAT contraption! How things change… I hate to admit that I don't even boil water on the stove any more – I use the microwave!

Be sure to occasionally look at life through the eyes of a child, and appreciate the wondrous things – natural and man-made – that exist in our world, so you don't ever take any of it for granted.

Overview

Myths to bust:

Myth #1:

Depression is just something that happens to us. We can't prevent or control it (other than medically for severe cases of depression) – we just have to let it run its course on its own.

Myth #2:

Complaining about a situation (to everyone with whom I have contact) will make it better.

Myth #3:

There's nothing I can do about the negative people in my life.

Myth #4:

I'm too cool to admit being awed by nature, technology or other awesome and awe-inspiring events.

What myths do I buy into?

____

____

How can I bust them?

____

____

Most common excuses we use to justify our fears and inactivity:

- I really don't care if I make myself feel worse!
- I don't care about anything any more – it really doesn't matter…
- I deserve to feel depressed!
- There's nothing I can do… it's out of my control.
- If it's meant to be, it will be (implied/hidden meaning: and I'm not going to do anything to help myself; I'll just wait for it to "be"!)

My "favorite" excuses used to justify my fears and inactivity:

Tips to overcome fear and take action:

1. Eliminate (or at the very least, reduce) contact with negative people in your life.

2. Recognize and eliminate your own negative thoughts and behaviors.

3. Allow yourself to mourn and/or vent, but don't let it go on too long.

4. Make a list of people who can help you get through your depression – and call on them when necessary.

5. Keep a "joke file" handy (either printed or electronic), so you can read and view funny materials – cartoons, jokes, cards – when you're feeling down or stressed.

6. Don't lose the wonder and enjoyment (even of very small things) that you had as a child. Look at the world through the eyes of a child to help you appreciate things you may be taking for granted.

Chapter Eight

Do I Really Have To...?

a.k.a. "Comfortable Enough" Can Be A Very Dangerous Place To Live

Why do people who hate their jobs remain in them for years, until one day they decide they can't take any more and walk away, finally determined to try something completely different?

Why do women stay with men who beat them, until one day the beating is so bad that they either die or realize they *will* die if they stay in that relationship?

Why do alcoholics and substance abusers keep abusing until one day a cataclysmic event causes them to reach bottom and either destroy themselves or get help and rehabilitate themselves?

Why does it often take a tremendous, destructive event in order for people to change their circumstances and reach for their dreams?

A tragic, or near-tragic, event forces people to reconsider the direction in which they're headed.

A tragic, or near-tragic, event forces people to reconsider what they're doing, and the direction they're headed. A heart attack suffered by one family member will often cause an entire family to re-focus and rearrange their priorities, at least temporarily. However, the more quickly the danger passes, the more quickly the lessons are forgotten as everything goes back to the way it was before the event.

Why is it so difficult to make permanent changes in our lives, even when those changes have the potential to greatly improve the quality of our lives?

I believe that in order to answer this question, we must first look at the way we view what we already have versus what we really want. This view affects our drive, our desire to change, our commitment level, what risks we are willing to take, and how persistent we will be in the face of temporary setbacks and failures.

Comfortable Enough

The crux of the problem is that although many of us have not yet fully realized our dreams, we are "comfortable enough". The insidious nature of "comfortable enough" or "good enough" can cause us to settle for less than what we really want in life.

Up to a certain point, the unsatisfying job is paying the bills and providing benefits, so we stay in it. In other cases, an unhealthy relationship may be providing a home, children, or income and is "tolerable" because of the other things it provides. Until a condition becomes so uncomfortable that the perceived benefits no longer outweigh the discomfort, we are usually not motivated to change any situation.

There are many reasons for this lack of motivation, most of which arise from our fear of the unknown.

Tempting Fate

We're afraid that if we try to change things for the better, they may actually get worse – or we may lose everything we've worked for up until now. It's as if we're afraid to ask for more or we'll be "punished" for being greedy. This is especially true if things are not exactly terrible, but just unfulfilling or unsatisfying in some way. It may even be reinforced by others around us who ask, "What more could you possibly want?" "Aren't you ever satisfied?"

These destructive questions and attitudes poison our society. Even worse, class envy, racism, sexism and other "plagues" also arise too often. We're so afraid to make our situations better because we don't want to be viewed as "the greedy rich", "better than" anyone else, or "trying to be someone we're not" that we subconsciously hold ourselves down – and allow others to hold us back because they're not in the position they want to be in, either. It's much easier to denigrate an entire class of people than to try to become successful and be accused of trying to become one of them, even if we're not.

No one has to be greedy to be rich. This is not a prerequisite. In fact, if we're rich, we can do an awful lot of good with the money at our disposal.

I have a friend who is black – and very successful in her career. Now that she's experiencing a higher level of success, some of her friends are accusing her of "trying to be white." She's not trying to be white! She's simply trying to be **successful**. This incomprehensible attitude strongly implies that her friends do not associate being successful with being black. Due to this self-limiting attitude, those she's leaving behind (mainly because they're not willing to work as hard for their own success as she is) are attempting to hold her back in order to feel better about themselves and their position.

If we'd just stop labeling people, we could actually do some good once we reached our goals.

We must all stop buying into societal pressures to be what others want us to be – and become what *we* want to be. If we'd just stop labeling people, we could actually do some good once we reached our goals – and more good would be done because more of us would actually reach our goals and feel good about doing so!

The Human Condition

The reasons why it is so difficult for us to motivate ourselves to change unsatisfactory situations, even when we want to, can be placed into four categories typical of the human condition. They encompass the fears and justifications given above, as well as others:

- Fear
- Procrastination
- Laziness
- Ignorance of All the Possibilities

Fear

Fear is, by far, the biggest reason we stop ourselves: fear of the unknown, fear of failure, fear of rejection, fear of appearing stupid, fear of embarrassment, and sometimes even fear of success.

Fear is not, in and of itself, a terrible thing. It sometimes stops us from doing things that will cause us harm. However, more often than not, fear stops us from trying anything new, simply because we don't know what the future holds if we try it. Our opinions of ourselves may be altered, others' opinions of us may be altered, or we may suffer the embarrassment of public or private failure.

If a fear is reasonable, we must react because of it. If it's not, we must act, despite it.

We must remember that fear is an element of our daily lives – it happens to everyone; no one is exempt. How we handle that fear determines how successful we will be in our lives. We must learn to accept the presence of fear, analyze why we're feeling it and whether it's reasonable or not – and determine the best course of action. If it's reasonable, we must react because of it. If it's not, we must act, despite it.

Procrastination

Procrastination has been called one of the greatest diseases of our society. This common human trait has caused more people to fail at their goals than almost any other.

There are many reasons why people procrastinate, even when the task being pushed off is one they really want to accomplish.

Some procrastinate because they really don't want to do the task at hand. This is certainly understandable. However, if we really dislike a task so much that we continually put off doing it, we actually cause ourselves more prolonged stress and anxiety over anticipation of doing the task than will actually result from just doing it. Once it's done, we're free to go on to more pleasant tasks.

Others procrastinate because they lack a sense of urgency to perform the task. They feel "there's always tomorrow". But when we're talking about achieving our dreams, tomorrow may never come and accomplishment of the dream gets pushed further and further into the future. Meanwhile, we are "stuck" in an unsatisfactory situation for a longer period of time.

A prime example of this is Harry Chapin's hit song, "Cat's in the Cradle", in which a boy continually asks his father to do things with him as he is growing up. The father is always too busy, saying, "Not today; I've got a lot to do." The verse continues, "When you coming home, Dad?" "I don't know when, but we'll get together then, son. You know we'll have a good time then." Predictably, the boy grows up, never actually getting that time with his father and becoming just like his Dad in the process. At one point in the song, the Dad is the one asking, "When you coming home, son?" "I don't know when, but we'll get together then, Dad. You know we'll have a good time then." The son now has no time for his father (or, as the song implies, for his own children), perpetuating a destructive cycle of always putting things off until tomorrow – which never comes.

In order to avoid looking back on our lives with regret, it is essential to learn as early as possible in life not to procrastinate on things that mean a lot to us. Participating in our children's lives, spending time with family and friends and accomplishing the financial and career goals that will fulfill and support us in the manner we desire are worthy of our time and effort. In fact, isn't that what we're doing all this for in the first place?

In addition, the song demonstrates just how much our children learn from us through example, whether or not we intentionally teach them these lessons.

Establishing the habit

The only way to avoid the "Procrastination Trap" is to establish a habit of action. If we get into the habit of taking action NOW – not at some nebulous point in the future, but right now – we begin to take control of our lives.

The sooner we establish a habit, the sooner it will become second nature to us. Just imagine – if we start now, we could be on our way to success in a short time! The longer we put off the necessary habits to get from point A to point B, the longer we must view ourselves as someone who hopes for success, instead of as an active participant in our own success story.

One of the biggest time-wasters is continually identifying and re-identifying a task that needs to be done, but never actually getting to it. Whether we're moving a newspaper, magazine, or other piece of paper from one pile to another on our desk (always planning to read it or otherwise "take care of it" later); or we're investigating several colleges but never actually applying to any; or we're gathering research before we start writing that book, article or speech – we're all guilty of procrastination over one thing or another.

We've got to learn to take care of that piece of paper by handling it one time, reading it and filing it or throwing it away, as appropriate. Let's face it: if you haven't done something with that pile that's been sitting on your desk for 6 months (and in fact you can't even remember everything that's in it), throw it away! At least you can make a clean start on the next pile! But take action now – and then try to do the same with everything new that comes your way.

The sooner we begin to act on our dreams, the sooner we will achieve them.

Laziness

Laziness is another plague of the human condition.

Allow me to clarify: we all get lazy *at times* – that's OK! We do not have to be busy every second of every waking hour each day! I don't agree with those who say we can't take some downtime and enjoy a TV show or movie we'd like to see. Those who say we must wisely utilize every single second of every day put an unreasonable burden on us ordinary humans, by making us feel guilty about taking a little time to rest, relax, unwind and/or pamper ourselves. Just because we're not reading a self-help book, listening to a motivational tape, or reading an industry or trade journal, newspaper or magazine doesn't mean we're wasting our precious time.

That's not to say we're supposed to sit like slugs in front of the TV for 10 hours a day, either! There is a balance. However, unless we give ourselves permission to unwind and relax sometimes, even "wasting" a few hours on what others might call "nonsense", we perpetuate the myth that every productive human being must be a complete workaholic who never wastes a second of any day.

Laziness is a problem if we continually:

- allow it to prevent us from doing necessary tasks for our betterment, our health or welfare or the health and welfare of others in our lives;
- take advantage of others' generosity and energy due to our laziness; or
- sabotage our success – or the success of others involved in mutual projects – because we're too lazy to keep our promises and hold up our end of the bargain.

Ignorance of All the Possibilities

Ignorance of all possibilities is what kept me from realizing my potential earlier in life. I was limited by my own experience. If I hadn't experienced a particular thing in my own life, I never really knew it existed. Even if I'd heard of it, if I hadn't seen proof of it in my own world, I didn't believe it was possible for me.

We must continually expand our horizons – and those of our children. If we never expose ourselves to the endless possibilities in the world, and do so for our children at an early age, those possibilities remain closed to us.

We owe it to ourselves and our families to broaden our horizons, experience new foods, new people, new cultures, learn about new products and ideas, research new career paths, look for support and help from others – and always ask for advice and answers to our questions. Only by being fully aware of all possibilities can we be the best prepared to achieve our dreams.

Also, if we broaden our horizons at an early age, new ideas will not be so foreign to us later in life – and we may be less tempted to take the "safe/known" road versus the one that will truly make us happy – when it really counts.

The "Safe" Road

My first career move to become a secretary marked the beginning of a 15-year journey of taking the "safe" road rather than the "risky" one. For years I remained in the safe "niche" I had carved out for myself, simply because it was one with which I was familiar because my mother had been a secretary – and a great one, at that! So, when I graduated from college, out of money to continue on and earn an advanced degree, I forced myself into that career because I typed fast and was very organized – two traits I knew would serve me well in that career – and because I didn't know what else I could, or should, do.

Just so there's no confusion, I want to point out that the administrative positions were not the problem. I know many wonderful secretaries (my mom included) who are the cornerstones of the businesses they serve. I was one, too! However, even though I was a very good secretary and enjoyed many aspects of that career, I always had to struggle to keep my voice hushed in the office, to be reserved most of the time, and to stifle many of the things that come naturally to me so I could fit well into the corporate mold. The problem was that I was not meant for the quiet corporate environment.

Predictably, the very traits I had to stifle in corporate positions are the ones that make my speaking career so successful and enjoyable! I now KNOW what I was meant to do – and I love doing it! When you reach that point, you'll know it. Until then, do everything to the best of your ability – not only so others can recognize it, benefit from it, and reward you for it, but so you know you've done your best in every situation – whether or not it's your intended long-term objective.

During these early years, I ventured occasionally into other career paths (mainly at the encouragement of others) but never stayed there, for one reason or another. I continued this pattern for years, always returning to what I knew when a change occurred, until I finally became so frustrated with myself and my lack of courage to try something different that I made a drastic change into sales – a change triggered by a simple comment from my real estate broker who said to me, "You know, you'd be a good real estate agent."

I laughed the first time she said it because I had NEVER pictured myself in any kind of sales position. However, when she repeated it, I was in such a desperately unhappy employment position that I decided it would be better to take the risk than to stay in the current position. Also, I respected her opinion and trusted her judgment. She saw something in me that I didn't see in myself. So, at age 38 I hung onto her belief in me like a lifeline and took the plunge!

I have never looked back, although I have sometimes lamented the 15 years I lost due to my lack of confidence to try something different. Whenever I begin to feel this way, I just thank God for getting me where I want to be before it was too late – and for helping me as I pursue my speaking and writing career.

I've often thought of the crossroads and decision points in my life, and realize now how I continually sabotaged myself when trying anything new. Opportunity after opportunity to break out of the mold arose, only to be discarded because it was too "risky".

The chart below illustrates my eventual progression from the safe to the risky path, as well as how dramatically my life and career changed once I opened my mind to new possibilities and took some calculated risks. You'll notice that, at a couple of points in my life, I *did* manage to take a different (even risky) road, but then retreated to the safe one when the next crossroad came up.

Choice(s) presented to me:	***Path taken:***
After graduating from college: continue with further education, or find a job doing what I knew I could do (secretarial)?	Secretary/Safe
Became interested in data processing; scored well on tests: become a System Librarian or remain a Secretary?	Secretary/Safe *(System Librarian job paid less and was a less known career path)*
Stay in a secretarial position or become a Business Systems Consultant (BSC)/Systems Analyst?	BSC/Relatively risky *(new field/career, but with steady pay, benefits and same parent company)*
Remain a BSC or go into a desktop publishing business with my mother (Write Touch)?	Write Touch/Relatively risky *(Entrepreneurial, but my mother had already established the business)*

Mom needed surgery and couldn't continue business: Go back to being a secretary or stay in business myself, possibly taking on a partner?	Secretary/Safe *(Staying in business myself was too scary; also, partnership with a stranger was too scary)*
Company moved too far to commute: Find another secretarial position or do something different?	Secretary/Safe *(Didn't know what else to do.)*
Unhappy in my job: Find another secretarial position or go into real estate	Real Estate/Very Risky *(Untried, entrepreneur≠ial, 100% commission-based sales, but high income potential and I could be my own boss!)*
Go into speaking and training with a business partner or stay in real estate	Speaking/Relatively risky *(Partner already had business up and running, but I had to leave a 6-figure income behind)*
Partnership ended at the end of one year: Go back to real estate or continue speaking	Speaking/Very Risky – *(Only one year of experience, very few contacts of my own, lower income and higher expenses – probably resulting in a net loss for a while)*

Looking at the choices I've made, it is obvious that it was not until relatively late in life that I began *consistently* making less safe/more risky career choices in order to pursue a goal I truly desired.

Early in my career, I sacrificed my dreams for the safe route. Later, I sacrificed "safeness" in order to do what I desired. What a shift! I would still be stuck in a position that wasn't right for me, if it hadn't been for this change in my thinking.

What decisions have you made?

Look back at the crossroads that have occurred in your life. Review how your decisions have changed, as you have grown. Observe how the situations that present themselves have changed over the years, and analyze your reaction to each situation as it arose. Which road(s) have you taken? Were they always the safe ones, regardless of the fact that they weren't the ones you really wanted to take – or have you taken some calculated risks along the way? Are you still taking the safe route, even when you didn't want to go that way?

Perhaps you can see some parallels to my life as you evaluate the decisions you've had to make. The older you are, the more decisions you've had to make. Are there situations right now in your life that require a decision on your part? Are you ready to take a carefully considered risk? Or will you always continue to take the "safe" path back to the familiar, the already-known?

I am living proof that people can change and grow, even after years of believing they have gone as far as they can go. I held myself in positions where I succeeded but was not fulfilled, simply because I didn't believe I could do more. I used every excuse in the book – and I became quite good at making them believable. This is why I demonstrate in each chapter of this book the most common excuses we use to hold ourselves back.

We must stop making excuses to justify our fears – and start living the lives we desire!

Before we get to the typical Overview for this chapter, I have provided a chart in which you can write down and analyze the decisions you've had to make in your life. Continue on a separate sheet of paper, if necessary. Approach this exercise with a critical and objective eye. If you're ever to change anything, you must first recognize and analyze your previous patterns. This will tell you if you've been progressing over time, or staying in the same risk (or risk-avoidance) pattern you've always used. Doing this exercise will allow you to recognize (and then implement) the changes necessary to achieve your dreams.

Choice(s) presented to me:	***Path taken:***

Overview

Myths to bust:

Myth #1:

If I ask for more, I'll be punished for being "greedy".

Myth #2:

I am the way I am, and I just can't control that.

Myth #3:

Women/men/young people/old people/blacks/whites (etc.) can't – or don't – do that!

Myth #4:

The [misguided] opinions of others should guide our actions and stop us from trying something different or new.

Myth #5:

If I watch TV, go to the movies, or read a novel occasionally, I'm a slug – completely wasting my valuable time on "nonsense"!

What myths do I buy into?

____

____

How can I bust them?

____

____

Most common excuses we use to justify our fears and inactivity:

- What I have now is good enough." "Things are good enough the way they are.
- If it was good enough for my parents, it's good enough for me!
- I don't want to tempt fate. I don't need any more than I've got now.
- People won't like me if I think of myself and go for my dreams.
- People will judge me for doing this, so I shouldn't do it.
- I can't do that – I've never done, or even seen, that before!
- I'm afraid to do that.
- I'll do it – first thing tomorrow!
- I just don't feel like doing it now.

My "favorite" excuses used to justify my fears and inactivity:

Tips to overcome fear and take action:

1. Don't discount someone else's remarks about your potential. They may actually see something legitimate in you that you don't see in yourself.

2. As you make more and more decisions, and begin to trust yourself and your instincts, take some calculated risks designed to get you on the path you desire, rather than simply further along the one you're on, even when it's not where you want to go.

3. Make a list of the careers you'd love to try. Then list the traits you possess that would help you in those careers. Also make a list of the traits you possess that will hinder you, so you can begin controlling and modifying those traits now, if necessary. (No one should try to be someone they really are not, but you can succeed, for example, in quiet environments, even if you're not quiet – or in ones that require you to be more outgoing, even if you're naturally shy.)

4. Stop labeling people and trying to fit them into certain molds. Be who you are – and encourage others to do the same.

Continued

5. Don't allow others to label you because of your dreams and desires. If they don't understand what you want to do, ignore their efforts to hold you back. Just because they're not where they want to be doesn't mean you have to stay unhappy and unfulfilled along with them.

6. Just because others are not fulfilling their dreams, that doesn't mean you shouldn't fulfill yours. You're not diminishing them if you fulfill your dreams. You're allowing them to diminish you if you don't try to achieve yours.

Chapter Nine

Real Men (and Women) Don't Have Dreams!

a.k.a. It's Not All Semantics

The Myth

Real men don't have dreams! And if they do have them, they certainly aren't about to share them in public – with actual *people*! Those who share this mindset suffer from the misguided notion that having – and especially sharing – dreams is a sign of weakness or vulnerability – or of being gay*. Many men are uncomfortable getting into that "touchy-feely" stuff. That's just for women! *("Hey, what's that quiche doing on my plate?!")* Add to this the fact that some very powerful women are now buying into this myth, believing that it will make them *appear* weak (at least in the eyes of their male counterparts) if they admit they have dreams, and an entire myth is propagated.

Let me ask a couple of questions: What about the small business owner who wants to take her business national? Or the CEO who wants his company to go global? What do you call these statements, if not dreams?

**There are many different kinds of labels. For example, If a man is assertive, he's a good leader. If a woman is assertive, she's a … well, we all know the label assigned to her.*

Pardon me – that's right. We call them goals. We don't call them dreams. We can't. Why? Because the word "dreams" has emotional connotations that are not traditionally acceptable in the business world, where most formal goal-setting is done.

It's completely acceptable – and even expected – for a big businessperson to have goals. The word "goal" is a sturdy, objective, dispassionate term, thereby making it acceptable in the unemotional world of business. If every ounce of emotion, passion or feeling is removed from a concept, it becomes an acceptable business term: goal, mission, objective.

However, if we take every ounce of passion out of whatever we want to accomplish – and look at it only in clinical or technical terms, how do we get excited about achieving our goals? How do we get excited about sharing them with others? More importantly, how do we get others excited about helping us accomplish them?

We must get over our discomfort with the word "dream" and allow ourselves to feel the full power of allowing our emotions to help us achieve them. Don't worry about labels designated by other people! Who cares what they say about you? I realize this is easier said than done; I've struggled with worrying about what others think most of my adult life, too. However, if someone is going to label you for any reason at all*, whose problem is it – yours or theirs? It appears to me that those who label others are the ones with a problem, not the other way around.

The difference between a goal and a dream

While, on the surface, this seems to be just a matter of simple semantics, I'd like to explain the differences between a goal and a dream.

**It's an ironic shame that our current and excessive focus on the gay issue (originally done in an effort to increase sensitivity and tolerance) seems to have had an adverse effect on straight men who may have become more willing to develop and show their sensitive side if it weren't for the fear of being labeled "gay".*

Dreams are what we are passionate about. Business dreams translate into powerful mission statements. Our dreams explain why we choose a certain career path over another; they're why we develop a women's clothing line instead of opening an ice cream shop or becoming an accountant. For example, when someone passionately wants to design affordable clothes that real women can wear (vs. what those skinny little teenage models wear all the time) to allow women to feel good about themselves and not break the bank in the process, that is a dream. When another person wants to discover a cure for cancer, that's another dream.

Dreams are the stuff happiness is made of! They spur us to action. Remembering and focusing on our dreams are what get us excited enough to act on them in the first place. They keep us motivated when we encounter obstacles and help us share our vision with others whose assistance we may need.

Goals do not! You can't get excited, or get your employees (or loved ones, in the case of a personal dream) excited about mere goals. You *can* get them excited enough about a dream to help you accomplish the goals necessary to reach it. But when they share your dream, your dream becomes their dream; consequently, your goals become their goals.

While goals are a very important part of achieving our dreams, they are simply the steps and sub-steps we must take to get from point A to point B, from point B to point C, and so on. They are the milestones on the way to the dream. The ultimate destination – point ZZZ – is the dream. It is only accomplished after each step in the process is completed. For example, I doubt that any successful businessperson would say that putting together a business plan and budget is one of their dreams! But they will acknowledge that it is an absolutely necessary step (or goal) in the process if they ever want to have a chance of achieving their dream of running a successful business.

Goals are task-oriented. They are often tedious chores, some with multiple steps that must be completed in a logical sequence. They are the items with the deadlines and the budgets, the necessary bread-and-butter items of any dream. But they are not the dream itself.

Many different dreams can – and often do – share the same standard goals. These same standard goals can be accomplished in pursuit of a virtually unlimited number of dreams.

For example, reputable charitable organizations all have the same basic goals: to raise money and keep expenses low. But their dreams are all different! One may be to find a cure for cancer or AIDS; another may be to help children experience their dreams before they die at a young age; a third may be to help battered women get out of abusive relationships.

Who gets excited about simply "raising money and keeping expenses low"? Would you ever get anyone to join you in these efforts if you didn't share with them *why* they would be doing it? Of course not! There's no point to it without the dream. The dreams are the *why* – the goals are simply the *how.*

By calling a dream simply a "goal", we deprive ourselves of the necessary emotion that allows us to become so energized and excited by it that we make a conscious decision to act on it. Without that energy and its accompanying action, we deprive ourselves of even the remotest possibility of achieving the dream.

Daydreaming vs. "having a dream"

Having a dream without having the energy or drive to accomplish it can be likened to daydreaming. It's interesting to note that most people will more readily admit to "daydreaming" than to "having a dream". Why?

First of all, no one will ridicule anyone for daydreaming. We've all done it! Daydreaming usually implies fantasizing about things we never expect to happen, such as winning the lottery, or being a huge sports star, musician or famous actor. Because daydreams are so far out of reach for us – and often are admittedly unrealistic because we have no musical or sports talent, nor do we buy lottery tickets – we are under no obligation to act on them. In fact, people would think we'd be crazy even to try most of them. They are fun breaks from reality that place no stress on us to achieve them. They are accepted as fantasy, and that's that.

However, "having a dream" implies that we will take action to accomplish it, thus exposing us to fear, ridicule and loss of self-esteem if we don't do what we set out to do. Having a dream, especially if we admit it to others, is a scary proposition. No one wants to feel like a loser. Although failing at an attempt at accomplishing a dream is far from qualifying us for the title "Loser", this is how we often feel – and how we sometimes allow others to make us feel. Thus, the temptation to deny having a dream is reinforced through the use of excuses and justifications in order to help us avoid the fear that accompanies any real dream.

"Having a dream" is taking a daydream to the level of action.

However, if more of us stopped simply daydreaming and started admitting that we have achievable real-world dreams, more of us would be happier with our lives!

A daydream is only out of reach if we don't take action to bring it within reach! "Having a dream" is taking a daydream to the level of action.

What's the difference between a daydream we'd never act on, and one that would spur us to action? There are three factors that will truly determine whether or not our dreams remain simply daydreams, or become real dreams deserving of the effort it will take to achieve them:

1. Is it physically possible?

Do I have the physical capability of making the dream come true? Whether it's physical ability, sports or musical talent, or any other natural ability, we must have it (in one form or another) in order to accomplish certain goals. Like it or not, there are certain physical limitations in certain areas that will cause us to fail if we attempt dreams that require something we just don't have. I will never be a basketball star if I have no height and no physical sports talent. I will never become a famous singer if I have no vocal talent.

This doesn't mean we shouldn't be creative in finding ways to make it possible. A terrific case in point is that of painters without arms, hands or fingers who create unbelievable masterpieces by holding a paintbrush in their teeth or their toes! In these cases, the artistic talent IS there – they've just had to be creative in finding ways to express it.

First and foremost we must have the talent and capability to accomplish the dream. We must determine whether or not we have it. Don't assume – give it a try. Then we must recognize and accept reality, whichever way it goes. If we don't, we will spend our lives chasing impossible dreams, rather than wisely using the talents we've been given to accomplish something that is possible.

2. Do I want it badly enough?

When all is said and done, we must want it badly enough to continue through adversity, ridicule and physical, emotional and financial threat. We must assume, up front, that it won't be an easy road or a swift one, especially if the dream is BIG! Analyzing how badly we want to achieve the dream is critical before we ever attempt it. If we don't want it badly enough, we may as well save ourselves the expense, trauma and time of doing something half-heartedly, only to quit halfway through when the going gets too tough for us to continue.

Keeping in mind the reason for wanting it that badly is crucial. When we can focus on the reason, the *why*, we allow ourselves to focus on what's important rather than the temporary setbacks that occur as we try to reach our dreams.

Remember this quote by the famous philosopher, Friedrich Nietzsche: "He who has a *why* can bear almost any *how*."

3. Do I believe it can be done – *by me*?

When many of us look at the success of other people, thus proving unequivocally that a certain accomplishment *can* be done, we shrug it off and say, "Yeah, sure he did it. He was born with a silver spoon in his mouth!"; or maybe we say, "Yes, but she just got lucky. I'm just not that lucky, so *I'd* never be able to do that!"

Unless we actually begin to believe that we also can accomplish even our wildest (and absolutely possible for us) dreams, we will never realize them. Until we stop using excuses that simply justify our fears and cause us not to try to accomplish our dreams, we will never truly believe that it's possible for us. We will continue to admit that it IS possible for other people – it's just not possible for us.

The magnitude of the dream

One problem I see when people begin to think about dreams is that many of us think immediately of Martin Luther King when we think of "dreams". All most of us have to do is simply hear the phrase "I have a dream" and we automatically think of Dr. King. This is not a bad thing, in and of itself. However, by doing this some of us inadvertently sabotage ourselves because we become very uncomfortable with accepting our own dreams as true dreams. It's as if a dream doesn't really qualify as a dream unless it's of the incredible magnitude of Martin Luther King's. We believe that since most of us will probably never do something that big, our dreams don't qualify and must not be worthy of the label.

Again, we're much more comfortable using, and reverting back to, the word "goal" to label what we want to do in life, not only because it's smaller in magnitude than an actual "dream", but because it probably won't require us to sacrifice as much.

Dreams require sacrifice; there's no getting around it. They may not require the ultimate sacrifice, as Dr. King's did, but make no mistake – we do have to sacrifice certain things to achieve them. The sooner we accept this fact and plan for the sacrifices we will have to make, the better our chances of achieving the dream. Once we determine how badly we want to achieve our dreams, we can determine what we would be willing to sacrifice in their pursuit – and for how long.

This is all part of the planning and goal-setting process that is necessary to accomplish the dream. Whether our dreams are large or small, they are ALL worthy of the label "dream". How much sacrifice, how much planning and how long it will take all depend on the magnitude of the dream.

The point is that you should never compare your dreams to anyone else's. Don't let anyone else compare them, either. You'll usually come up short, at least in your own mind. Accept your dreams for what they are – accomplishments that are important to you. Then go about making the necessary plans to begin, and then accomplish, them.

Isn't it all semantics?

No! It is not all semantics. In fact, calling dreams goals, just so we don't look "vulnerable" or "weak" by admitting we have them is the ultimate in sabotaging ourselves through semantics.

I'd like you to try an exercise right now: say the following two sentences out loud, one at a time, allowing yourself to analyze your feelings about each one. (It's even better if you can do this exercise with someone else and say the sentences to that person, then get their feelings and reactions to each sentence and how you said them.)

The first sentence is, *"I have a goal."* Say it like you mean it. How does that feel? For many, it will simply be a statement of fact. For some, it will be a fallacy since many of us were never taught to do proper goal-setting; for others, it's been a while since they've set goals. Does this sentence conjure up any particular feelings? Do you smile when you say this statement? Do you feel like smiling?

Now say the sentence, *"I have a dream."* Again, say it like you mean it.

Did it feel any differently to you? Did you draw out the "m" in dream – or possibly the whole word itself? Didn't it feel like it needed to be said a little stronger, with a little more emphasis?

You may have felt a little discomfort saying this sentence. That very discomfort tells you that you do feel differently about the word dream than you do about the word goal. Did the person to whom you said it notice anything different? Was there anything different about your facial expression, the tone of your voice, even the size of your smile? You may also have giggled or laughed after saying it – or *while* saying it. Maybe you even imitated Dr. Martin Luther King as you said it, in an effort to use humor as a defense mechanism to hide your discomfort.

If you've done this exercise in the true spirit of experimentation and objective analysis, you will notice that you probably felt differently about the words you said, with more positive feeling, more emphasis and more weight given to the word "dream" than to the word "goal".

This is a very simple exercise, but it proves a complex and sizeable point. What if we started viewing our dreams as exactly that – dreams. Would you rather put more emotional expression and passion into your life, or reduce every aspect down to its least impactful terms?

What if we did this in our everyday lives? What if we took all the passion out of lovemaking… what would it be then? Simply meaningless S-E-X! Instead of an expression of love between two people passionately committed to each other, it would be reduced to a biological, clinical act. In fact, this is already happening in our society and I believe it's why we have so many problems in this area. By taking all meaning out of it, it becomes possible to just do it without thinking about it. This is what we're teaching our children!

Why do so many teens have sex at such an early age? Because we haven't taught them that it is a passionate, meaningful event that is to be saved for the right person. It's just a plain old act for which we hand out condoms and pills to prevent unwanted side effects like pregnancy and STDs. It's as if sex is such a non-event that a pamphlet, a condom and a pill will handle all aspects of what should be one of the most meaningful and seriously considered events of their lives.

If this is what's happening in critical areas of our personal lives, how can it be good for our professional lives? Wasn't it just a short while ago that we thought higher sales could be obtained by simply throwing a product into the market and hoping the public would buy it? If it was a good product, the public probably did buy it. However, soon everyone is producing the same – or an improved version of the same – product, creating fierce competition.

What we have discovered about sales and customer service, if nothing else, is that creating an exceptional experience for our customers (in other words, touching them on every level – emotionally, intellectually and physically) creates such loyal customers that no one can tear them away. At this point, the product itself takes on less importance than the experience customers have with the company. In other words, what touches their emotions becomes more important than the actual product. Not only that, but those customers then become cheerleaders for us, telling everyone they know about their experience and encouraging their friends and family to try us, too! This is how word-of-mouth operates – on emotions!

Causing emotional reactions, and becoming passionate about serving and exciting our customers does what plain-old products and services could never do! It causes such a strong reaction in our customers that they feel compelled to do something positive about it, sharing an exciting and gratifying experience with their friends, and wanting their friends to experience the same excitement and joy they felt.

It also creates loyal employees. We often hear employers bemoaning the fact that "it's so hard to get good help nowadays." Perhaps the real reason it's so hard to get employees to perform to our standards is that we have taken so much passion and excitement from their professional situation that they no longer feel a part of something vital or important. We're not passionate about what we do; we certainly don't share our passion with employees; therefore, they look at the position as just another job meant to hold them over only until they discover "what they really want to do." If we can tie our passion to theirs, they may discover that working for – actually *with* – us is what they really want to do.

The same principle holds true in our personal lives. Without the passion to create excitement about achieving our dreams, we will neither accomplish them alone nor create loyal friends dedicated to helping us accomplish them.

Let's take a lesson from this, and start calling our dreams what they are, and never call a dream a goal, or vice versa, again.

Overview

Myths to bust:

Myth #1:

Real men don't have dreams! And if they do have them, they certainly aren't about to share them in public – with actual *people*!

Myth #2:

Having dreams is a sign of weakness.

Myth #3:

A goal and a dream are the same thing. There is no reason to use one word over another.

What myths do I buy into?

___

___

How can I bust them?

___

___

Most common excuses we use to justify our fears and inactivity:

- I don't need help from anyone
- I couldn't get help from anyone
- You just can't get good help nowadays!
- I can do it faster, better, easier myself!

My "favorite" excuses used to justify my fears and inactivity:

Tips to overcome fear and take action:

1. By calling a dream simply a "goal", we deprive ourselves of the necessary emotion that allows us to become so energized and excited by it that we make a conscious decision to act on it. Put the passion back in your words, and allow that passion to carry you forward toward accomplishing your dreams.

2. A daydream is only out of reach if we don't take action to make it come within reach! Take action to turn your daydreams into real-life dreams.

3. Dreams require sacrifice. The sooner we accept this fact and plan for the sacrifices we will have to make, the better our chances of achieving the dream. Decide what you will sacrifice, and for how long, in order to achieve your dreams. Gain buy-in from others who must sacrifice with you, and keep your promise to yourself (and them) regarding the severity and length of the sacrifice.

Reader Exercises

1. What is my dream?

2. Is it actually possible? Why, or why not? (REAL reasons, if why not – not excuses!)

3. Why do I want to accomplish it?

4. How badly do I want to accomplish it?

5. What am I willing to sacrifice in order to achieve my dream?

Chapter Ten

Not For Women Only

a.k.a. Support Each Others' Dreams

Before we start, please don't assume I will be "man-bashing" in this chapter. That's not what this chapter is about. In fact, some of the ideas and beliefs discussed are held by women as well as men. Men and women alike must eliminate these limiting beliefs before they and their families can truly prosper.

Many women are currently attempting to either get a new career off the ground, or make more of their current career. They take themselves and their careers very seriously. Unfortunately, spouses and significant others (male and female) sometimes do not. Additionally, often a mother, sibling, other relative, or friend also holds a limiting belief system that hinders a woman from achieving the success she desires.

These significant others will often use statements such as, "Oh, quit playing around and get a *real* job!" or "Why are you taking money away from the family for this nonsense? It will never amount to anything. You're taking food out of your children's mouths and hurting the family!" Or, even worse, "You don't want to show your husband up, do you? Don't you want to be a good wife?"

If your first reaction to reading these words is, "Oh, come on – no one really thinks that any more!", think again. I am alarmed at the number of women I have met (and coached) in the years 2000 and beyond who face these attitudes on a daily basis. Some make it through and achieve their goals despite these obstacles; many don't, having lost the will to continue the constant struggle against such powerful negative emotions in their daily lives.

In this age of "enlightenment", I am astonished by the amount of self-limiting thinking that still goes on in our world. I can only imagine that it must be the same feeling minority groups have regarding the amount of racism that still occurs in the U.S. so many years after the Civil Rights movement began.

I have identified various types of scenarios I have encountered, as well as the phrases that characterize them, and listed them below to help others recognize when they may be in these situations, since we can only change a situation if we recognize and accept that we may be participating in it.

There may be others, but below is a list of the top 5 limiting beliefs I've seen that hold women back:

1. Women are just "playing around" in their careers; men are the *real* breadwinners of the family.
2. Women who make more money than their husbands are "showing their husbands up".
3. Women should be happy taking care of their husbands and children, even after the children are grown. They shouldn't need other outside interests.
4. Women should put their families above any other personal and professional goals.
5. And on the flip side: The goals of women who want to stay home to raise their children and care for their families are not

as worthwhile as those of women who desire a career outside the home.

Let's take a more in-depth look at each of these beliefs.

Limiting Belief #1: Women are just "playing around" in their careers; men are the *real* breadwinners of the family

Many factors contribute to this belief, including:

- Up-front societal and self-expectations
- Peer pressure
- Peripheral duties
- Limitations regarding the "right" field for women

Up-front societal and self-expectations

Most men are brought up believing they can (in fact, *must*) survive on their own. More importantly, they are taught that they are to be responsible not only for themselves, but for their wives and families as well. They must fulfill their duty, their place, their *destiny* as the "head of the family", the breadwinner, the decision-maker.

Since men are expected to be the "breadwinners" and to go on and do great things outside the home, expectations of the women in the family, and consequently a woman's expectations of herself, are much lower than they are for a man, right from the start. When a woman doesn't achieve great things outside her family, no one is surprised – or disappointed. In fact, when she does not play the largest role and achieve great things *within* the family environment, people are surprised and disappointed. Hence, the birth of the myth of needing to be "Super Woman", who if she wants a successful career outside the home, must still fulfill the largest role within the family in addition to her other "outside interests."

This may be a contributing factor to the fact that women making it big in the corporate and/or sales worlds are still bigger news than men doing the same thing (unless they have some great entertainment talent, such as a beautiful singing voice, great acting talent, or great writing talent). It is certainly a contributing factor to the rise in health problems for working women, such as heart attacks and ulcers.

This mindset is reinforced in every medium, including TV and movies. For example, we've all seen the old Westerns where the father dies, and the oldest son is told, "Well, you're the man of the family now – it's up to you." Even if he's only 10 years old!! The weight of the world is now placed upon a child, rather than on the remaining competent adult in the family – the mother!

What about her? She's often portrayed as helpless and clueless when it comes to how the family will be provided for financially. Occasionally, you'll see a story about the rare "strong" and exceptional woman who makes a name for herself (the novel "A Woman of Substance" comes to mind) and becomes rich, triumphing in the face of adversity. It continues, even in today's movies. I swear if I see one more woman trip over her own two feet while running away from the bad guys, thus slowing down the man who must come to her rescue, I will "suffer from the vapors" myself!

Given this type of programming, we see how it would be difficult for many men to relinquish authority (or any portion thereof) over what happens to the family, the money, etc. and allow a woman to make business and/or financial decisions that will affect the family income. The fallacy that doing so constitutes a show of weakness, indicating that you're just not a "real man" if you can't or don't provide for your family is still very strongly promoted in our society.

Peer Pressure

The peer pressure alone for a man to "be a real man" (or at least act like one in front of other real men) is also astounding. What happens when a man allows his wife to make decisions for him or their family (sometimes even for herself)? It often invites comments from other men (usually to his face, but occasionally behind his back as well), such as, "Who wears the pants in YOUR family anyway?" or "OK, now you can stand in the 'henpecked husband' line!" [We've all heard the joke about the line of men waiting at two doors to get into Heaven. One door is entitled "Henpecked Husbands" and has a long line of men in front of it. The other, which has just one man standing there, is marked "Independent Men". Finally, one of the men in the "Henpecked Husbands" line can't stand it any more and shouts over to the lone man, "Hey, how'd you do it? How did you get to be an independent man?" The lone man replies, "I don't know; my wife told me to stand here!"] While we can all appreciate the humor in this cartoon, it does make a statement about men who do what their women tell (or even simply ask) them to do.

Peripheral Duties

A further complication primarily affecting women is the issue of child care. Although many men now willingly step up and assume more child-rearing duties, most men still don't have to deal with this issue if they don't want to. Either way, it's still their choice. If they don't choose to help, there is no stigma attached to their actions. Many simply don their coats and leave for work each morning while their spouse takes care of the children. This happens regardless of whether or not she has a career outside the home. It is a reality for most people with children that childcare responsibilities still reside largely in the domain of the women in the household. If someone needs to take time off from a job to take children to a doctor, pick them up from school, or make other arrangements for their care and transportation issues, often it is up to the female partner.

The solution to this is to have open discussions regarding this issue, preferably before the children are born, so that the decision can be made as to who assumes which roles, based on availability and opportunity rather than previously-held assumptions.

Limitations regarding the "right" field for women

While I don't buy in to the notion that every field is right for every woman, there are relatively few fields where most women cannot compete on an even footing. We have to admit that certain fields involving physical attributes and abilities are obviously not equal (although there are exceptions to every rule). However, for most careers, women are equally capable of succeeding as their male counterparts, if given the opportunity to do so.

While much progress has been made in the workplace regarding these opportunities, there are still factors at work in the home that could hinder a woman's success. By the way, many of these factors also work in reverse, hindering a man's progress due to lack of support from significant others.

A woman (or man) who is successful in sales has one of the biggest opportunities in the entire career continuum for growth and financial prosperity. However, there is little question that if push comes to shove, she will usually be the one to sacrifice her career "for the good of the family" vs. the man doing so. This is true, even if he's in a dead-end job, or has to work multiple jobs just to hold the family together. What sense does this make? None! And yet, it still happens far too often.

Stay-at-home fatherhood and working motherhood are not for everyone. But we must realize that these dynamics are in play when questions arise from a woman's choice of career - or from her choice to even have a career!

People who believe that a woman trying to get a career off the ground is "just playing around" and "not contributing to the family" are suffering from serious misconceptions about what she is actually trying to do, as well as the benefits that could result from her actions. I remember one case in particular of a woman in a sales career whose husband made very little income at his job. She was fairly new at sales and needed a little more time and money, as well as practice at her profession in order to succeed; she began sales coaching with me.

Through her coaching sessions, I could see that she had the potential to be a top producer – if she got the chance. Unfortunately, her husband was so obsessed with the notion that he was the *real* breadwinner, and that she was simply "sucking vital income from the family pocketbook" that he badgered and belittled her every day to "get a real job, instead of costing the family more money." Due to his firm belief that he was the primary breadwinner, he considered his wife's activities superfluous, and therefore not worth spending valuable dollars to accomplish. In his mind, they should both focus on how *he* could earn more money.

One possibility under consideration was for him to take on another job which would have taken him away from his family more often and contributed an insignificant amount of extra money in the process. In addition, she was to work in a different position, one with a steady (albeit much smaller) paycheck, rather than try to succeed in her chosen career. What he refused to realize or admit was that his wife's career could have provided for them so handsomely that her husband could have quit all his jobs, and the family would still have been more financially stable – not to mention the fact that at least one parent would be spending more time with their children if he had allowed this scenario to occur.

I don't know what eventually happened to this woman. I do know that, out of despondence and frustration, she quit her coaching shortly after she began. Due to her husband's constant badgering, she was also on the verge of quitting her sales job and getting a different, much less financially and emotionally rewarding, job just because it came with a steady (although much smaller) paycheck.

Another colleague of mine was a promising saleswoman who, under the same kind of pressure from her husband, quit her sales job (for which she was on track to earn over $50,000 in her 2nd year in sales) and took a part-time position at a cosmetics counter in a mall store. Again, please don't get me wrong. There is absolutely nothing wrong with cosmetic counter jobs; there is, however, something definitely wrong with one person forcing another to abandon a career she enjoys and at which she is having success, simply to switch to a career with different guidelines and rules regarding having a steady paycheck so *he* feels better (and more in control).

Another woman I know was constantly pressured by her husband to "stop all her extracurricular activities" because he wanted her to stay home every night with him. These extracurricular activities were mainly after-hours networking events she attended to promote her new business and build awareness of her services in her community. Effective networking, especially at the beginning of a new business, is crucial in order to build the business quickly. This woman's husband was so adamant about her being home at night that he made her life miserable as she tried to build a business doing what she loved to do!

The sad fact is that if he were self-employed, and had to network after hours until his business got off the ground, he'd likely deem these same activities necessary and vital to the success of his business. If his wife had complained about being left alone at home while he was at these events, he would have tried to explain to her how necessary networking activities are for a new business; in addition, he would probably have become very frustrated and upset *with her* if she refused to understand or attempted to make him feel guilty about not being home with her.

However, when his wife attempted these activities, he considered it a disruption of his family life. Thus, he attempted to force her into providing him with the family framework he desired rather than sacrificing anything in the short term to foster their mutual long-term success as a family.

The scenarios happen more often than I care to recall. I have heard countless variations on these themes, and am saddened by the fact that these attitudes are still so prevalent in today's "enlightened" society.

When this situation occurs, it demoralizes a person, causing her to lose interest in trying to change or better her situation. It causes her to "settle" for less than she desires, simply because she gets little or no support for what she really wants to accomplish. Often she is actually forced to abandon her dreams by a significant person in her life in order to do something the other person deems more suitable.

The reasons for the badgering vary, ranging from the fact that a particular career doesn't fit that person's image of what a woman should do, to simple insecurity and jealousy, to the fact that a different job may bring in extra cash in the short term. It doesn't matter that the abandoned career could have brought in a lot of extra cash in the long term, in addition to immense joy and personal satisfaction. Focusing solely on immediate results destroys the long-term vision necessary to see future benefits.

Focusing solely on immediate results destroys the long-term vision necessary to see future benefits.

On the other hand, a man attempting to accomplish his dream is rarely spoken to, or even thought of, in this manner. He is deemed a hero for trying to better his situation for his family. Everyone agrees he should be encouraged along the way, no matter how successful – or unsuccessful – he is. Since the man is considered the real breadwinner, all his efforts at a career are tolerated and encouraged. Some men try for years to accomplish a dream, at the expense of everyone around them. Some succeed; others are always looking for that "lucky break", never taking their destiny in their own hands but simply waiting and hoping for something big to happen. In the meantime, he and his family drift haplessly on a sea of poverty and despair.

Why is it that a man engaging in this type of activity is trying to "better himself", while a woman engaging in the same activity is "playing around and hurting the family"?

Just imagine how a man would react to having these attitudes directed toward him while trying to provide for his family. It would completely demoralize him. There is a term for this type of activity: "emasculate". The term is described in the dictionary in two ways. One definition concerns *the physical act of depriving a male the option to reproduce.* The other concerns the societal definition, the one in which we are interested: *"to destroy the strength or force of; to weaken".*

Why is there no corresponding term for the same type of activity directed at women? There are general concepts and terms available, such as "demoralize" or "demotivate", but I have often wondered why there is no specific term that encapsulates the full meaning and devastation of these actions toward women, as there is for men. Sometimes people trivialize the contributions of at-home moms because they "don't bring in any money to the family." On the other hand, when women try to bring in money by getting outside jobs (especially if the job is non-traditional and/or risky in nature), their actions are often deemed superfluous, unnecessary and disruptive.

Until society realizes that the concept of "emasculation" can also apply to women, describing actions that strip them of their unique identity, gifts, strengths and value to themselves and their families, no concept will ever be able to fully describe their devastating effects. Perhaps we should coin a new term to describe these actions: "defeminate".

Maybe I'm being idealistic by believing a term can make such an impact. However, I ask you to think of how you feel when you simply hear the term "emasculate". It conjures up a whole range of negative feelings, doesn't it? We cringe when we think of (or see) this being done to a man. We hope never to do this ourselves to any man. Men and women alike understand the term and its implications, and all agree it is extremely undesirable. It is possible that by coining the term, attention will be called to the problem, a definition of these actions as a set of undesirable activities can be agreed upon, and eventually everyone will cringe when they think of these things being done to a woman.

In fact, we have all seen evidence that once society accepts a powerful and meaningful term for a condition or action, we can understand the term and its effects, recognize the problems inherent in pursuing these types of activities, and eliminate them. I liken this concept to medical and psychological conditions. Until you know what you're dealing with (in other words, scientists come up with a term for the condition, as well as a set of specific symptoms, causes and possible cures), people simply don't realize 1) that it exists at all; 2) that other people recognize and accept that it exists; 3) how it can be dealt with and cured; or 4) how it can be prevented in the future.

For example, until Chronic Fatigue Syndrome was defined, the term coined and possible treatments identified, most doctors didn't realize what they were dealing with, misdiagnosing and wrongly treating it. In fact, despite the fact that many doctors now recognize and treat the condition, there are still some doctors who won't admit it exists! I believe this will eventually change; however, in the meantime, we're moving in the right direction toward identification, diagnosis and treatment.

The same is possible for the concept of "defemination"...

Limiting Belief #2: Women who make more money than their husbands are "showing them up"

Since men are taught that they must be the primary breadwinners (or they're not real men), many men are threatened when *any* woman (but *especially* "his" woman) makes more money than he does.

A perfect example of this type of traditional thinking occurred in my own (very traditional Italian) family at a Christmas party one year. At that time, my husband and I had been married for 15 years, and in all that time I had never made more money in one year than he had. At the time of this party I had been a real estate agent for a couple of years and, for the first time in my life, had broken the $100,000 barrier! I didn't even mention the amount of money I had made, but just commented to one of my cousins that I made more money than Bruce (my husband) did the previous year. She immediately covered her mouth, gently hit me on the arm to admonish me, looked nervously at Bruce, and said, "Oh, my God – don't embarrass him like that!" Bruce just put a big smile on his face and said, "What do you mean? I'm LOVING this!!" And he turned to me and said, "Honey, when can I retire?"

Men and women – do you think you're more enlightened than this scenario portrays? Let's do a little visualization exercise. Men, you know what you make on a yearly basis. Picture yourself telling your accountant what you made last year, so he/she can prepare your taxes. Now, picture the woman in your life telling your accountant that she made $50,000 more than you did. How does this make you feel? Be honest!! Or, picture my party scenario where you don't even have to reveal how much money each of you made, just reveal the fact that your wife/girlfriend makes more than you do? How do people around you react? How do you feel? In financial terms, the overall picture may be terrific, but how does it feel in terms of conventional pride? Pride can, and does, cause a lot of unnecessary problems.

Luckily, I have an extremely supportive husband, who has no problem with the amount of money either of us makes, because it all goes into the same pot and we both benefit from the collective fruits of our labor! Maybe he wouldn't have been so supportive if I had not shared my income with him, but our decision as a couple is that everything is shared. That's how we work best! And he has no ego issues as to who makes the most, as long as we make and share it together.

Most women who enjoy a satisfying career do not do it simply to show up any man in particular – or men in general. While there are undoubtedly women for whom this is an added "benefit", most women do not make it their life purpose to show up their male counterparts.

Most women who have taken up careers have done so for the traditional reasons that men choose careers they will enjoy: either they need to work to help support the family, or they want to do something that will bring added fulfillment, satisfaction and the reward of a job well done to their lives. Many women admirably accomplish this through raising healthy, well-adjusted children in a loving family environment. A wonderful trend nowadays is that many men are also contributing to the emotional health of the family by being around and available to their children and spouses more often than in the past.

However, many women either want something more, or want something after their children have (very predictably) grown up and moved out of the home. After the children leave, most men have no disruption in their lives because they still have their jobs, which have always taken up the largest portion of their day during the workweek, and will continue to do so. Nothing is different for them once their children have moved out of the house.

For a woman who has focused her efforts either largely or solely on raising the children and being there for them, it is quite a different story. Now, seemingly her "reason for being" no longer exists, and she may begin to feel superfluous or useless as her role in her children's lives diminishes. Without something fulfilling and rewarding to take the place of the activities upon which she has previously based her life, she may begin to feel depressed and lonely, feeling that no one needs or loves her, and that it doesn't matter if she stays or disappears.

I believe this is one reason why so many marriages have problems after 25 or 30 years of "apparent bliss". The main focus of the woman's life has now changed, and discomfort sets in as she tries to find a new purpose and role in the family. She is supremely uncomfortable and uncertain about her role for the first time in her marriage; in addition, her husband is uncertain about what to do and often becomes uncomfortable because he feels unable to "fix" the problem. She may need more attention, but this doesn't mean that he has any more time to accommodate her new needs, nor should she rely solely on him to occupy the extra time she has on her hands. Many unusual and/or uncomfortable situations arise from the altered life pattern. Many couples make it through this transitional period by exercising a lot of patience and effort with each other. Many do not.

This situation can be compared to another common problematic "turning point", the retirement of one or both parties in the couple, as they now both have time on their hands and spend much more time together on a daily basis than they are accustomed to spending. One gets in the other's way as their routines are disrupted and changed. A period of adjustment must occur in order for couples to make it through these times. Each member of the family must be committed to the necessary changes in lifestyle, income, routines – and much more – in order to successfully make it through these times together.

Whether one or both parties are changing, it is only by creating a win-win situation that couples come through the change whole and can actually achieve a better situation afterward.

Limiting Belief #3: Women should be happy just taking care of their husbands and children, even after the children are grown. They shouldn't need other outside interests.

First of all, let me make it clear that this statement does not just pertain to women pursuing an outside career. It refers to the belief that women shouldn't have, or need, outside social interactions, career-related or otherwise, in addition to their family duties and routines.

Just think of the absurdity of this belief! Yet, many men believe that their wives should be happy just filling their family role. Worse, many women feel there must be something wrong with them if they don't feel satisfied with this one role in their lives, feeling guilty about wanting something more! This feeling of guilt is perpetuated and worsened if their spouse discourages them from even thinking about doing more, or berates them when they try to do so.

Human beings are social animals, and most of us enjoy the company of other people – even if not a lot of other people! We crave social interaction and variety in our daily lives. We need distraction from the performance of the same few activities day after day after day, without end.

Why do people have friends? Why do we keep in touch with our extended families? Why do neighbors seek each other out? Why do people join groups and associations? Or throw parties? Because we all feel a need for social interactions with other people.

When my husband and I first moved to Florida, I felt a tremendous sense of isolation when I began my speaking career on my own. My entire family was living far from me; my neighbors were very busy with their children and their lives; I worked alone from my home. My husband worked at an office two hours from our home, so he put in very long days between working and traveling to work. I didn't know anyone in the area where I lived and began to feel very lonely.

My husband, who is a very compassionate and understanding man, couldn't understand my loneliness. He wasn't feeling the same things I was, and couldn't understand why – until I brought a couple of details to his attention.

First, he worked in a large office and had formed friendships with people he saw there on a regular basis, enjoying social conversations with them before and after work, and during lunch. I worked alone all day.

In addition, he plays basketball twice a week in our local area. When I pointed out the fact that he had social interaction with these other men, he at first denied that it was social at all, claiming that it was "just playing basketball". So, I asked him if he really likes playing basketball. He admitted that he loves it, and feels deprived whenever it rains during basketball time, forcing them to cancel their games, which are held outdoors. Upon being asked if he liked the guys he played basketball with, he readily admitted that he did. They would talk before and after the games, and while they were stretching and warming up…

Suddenly, the light came on for him, as he began to understand that it wasn't just about exercising or "just playing basketball". It was about doing an activity that he really loved doing, meeting and talking to other people, forming friendships with them, and providing variety to his life other than just going to work, coming home, eating dinner, talking with me, watching a little TV and going to bed – and then doing it all over again and again, day after day.

Men are not the only ones who need this type of variety in their lives. Women also need and crave social interaction with other people, possibly even more than men! They need to form friendships and add variety to their day, rather than simply taking care of and conversing with small children, cooking and cleaning (in essence, their jobs during the day) and then eating dinner, talking to their husbands or watching a little TV and going to bed – and then doing it all over again and again and again, day after day.

So why does this limiting belief still exist? Why would any man expect this to be enough for his wife or significant other? And why would any woman beat herself up for not being satisfied with this situation?

I believe it's because these beliefs have been around so long, they are ingrained in us. They are now habits: that's the way it's always been, and that's the way it should be. Women who attempt to break the mold are not "good women" or "good wives" – they want too much; they should be happy with what they've got and stop rocking the boat! Whenever women do try to break these habits, these are the types of comments they often hear. It is very difficult to do something different when faced with the fierce guilt thrust upon them for not conforming.

If you don't believe this attitude is still around, or that some men believe that women's needs are more inconsequential than men's, just listen to some of the terms men use to describe women's social groups and activities: the koffee klatch; the hen party (I was horrified and highly insulted when I recently heard this one for the first time!); a bunch of cackling women; women's "little get-togethers"; and more. These terms describe more about the attitudes of the people who use them than they may be aware of.

Limiting Belief #4: Women should put their families above any other personal and professional goals.

While everyone (men and women alike) in a committed relationship should make that relationship, as well as other family relationships, a top priority, this belief should be an overall long-term *value*, not a statement for limiting *every moment of a person's life*. Nor should it be used as a weapon designed to control a person's every thought and action.

Too often, this worthwhile value is twisted in order to control others, manipulating them to abide by the wishes of another, or used in an effort to control their daily activities. Many women (and some men) are controlled by domineering partners who use this method of "manipulation through guilt". The domineering partner is free to do whatever he or she wishes, while the controlled partner is expected to always put the other person, as well as the family (and often the extended family) first in an effort to prove they really care about the family.

This method is frequently used whenever the non-domineering partner attempts to do something for herself, such as make friends outside the immediate family, join a club, go back to school, volunteer for charitable work or get a job. Guilt-inducing statements are used to discourage any attempt at individualization or independence, because these actions cannot be tolerated by a domineering partner who fears losing control over the other person.

Limiting Belief #5: The goals of women who want to stay home to raise their children and care for their families are not as worthwhile as those of women who desire a career outside the home.

Unfortunately, many of the people who hold this belief and judge others by it, are women. Whether it's a form of self-defense to justify their own desire to work out of the home, or a misguided belief instilled in them at an early age by someone else, this belief too must stop! All women are entitled to choose whatever path they desire – and all paths are equally worthy when it comes to fulfilling those dreams. No one needs to judge or be judged on these criteria.

Since when is this a lesser choice? Children are our future leaders and contributing members of society. If anything, the lack of a loving, caring parent in the home has caused more harm than good in our modern society. Women who make this choice today, even in the face of pressure to "be more" or "do more" than that, are to be commended for their courage to stand up and do what they believe is right for themselves and their families.

What can we do about these attitudes?

1. *Recognize that they do exist.*

   As the first rule of Alcoholics Anonymous states, if you're not aware of the problem, and don't admit to it, you can't fix it.

2. *Talk to the other person about the fact that he or she seems to promote one or more of these attitudes.*

If someone important in your life holds one or more of these beliefs, you must make him or her aware of it. He may not consciously realize what he believes or says to you. Give him the benefit of the doubt and attempt first to point out the limiting beliefs. Tell him how it negatively affects you and/or your family when he acts in accordance with those beliefs.

3. *Gain a commitment from the other person to change these beliefs, as well as her actions toward you.*

   Once a person is made aware of her beliefs and actions, try to gain a commitment from that person to change. Even if her beliefs don't change immediately, try to get her to change her outward actions toward you. The change in beliefs may take longer, but if you ask for a change in behavior, requesting at least "tolerance" of the changes you'd like to attempt, she may be more open to this. Don't expect it to be easy or quick! Some of these beliefs are so ingrained and have been part of a person's life for so long, it may be difficult for that person to change. Expect good days and bad days, setbacks and advances. But you must at least try to get everyone involved moving in the same direction as harmoniously as possible.

4. *If you can't get the other person to accept your opinions and at least attempt to change, seek professional help.*

   It is no shame to seek professional help when you can't overcome a particular obstacle. So many of us feel inadequate when we have to ask others for help, especially professional help where we're afraid of being labeled, that we try to handle everything ourselves. Some situations cannot be handled without outside, objective assistance. Don't be so afraid to enlist help that you settle for less, or worse, allow the relationship to deteriorate to the point where it is irreconcilable.

5. *Stop the negative self-talk. Seek professional help, if necessary.*

   If you are the one who holds a self-limiting belief, you must begin to change your own attitudes and opinions. This is not an easy task, so don't beat yourself up if at first you don't succeed. Keep trying to recognize when you're reinforcing the wrong belief and make efforts to eliminate those actions and reactions when they occur.

6. *Recite positive affirmations that reinforce the beliefs you wish to hold.*

   Positive affirmations are statements, made in the present tense, that affirm a belief or attitude you want to reinforce. For example, "I am a successful woman, deserving of all the abundance life has to offer," or "I am a successful businesswoman. I work with many satisfied clients whom I help improve their businesses and their personal lives." At first, it may feel uncomfortable, as the statements may feel "untrue", but you must say these statements forcefully, AS IF you believe them now, in order to convince your subconscious mind that they are true. Your subconscious mind believes what you tell it. In order to change the beliefs, you must change the self-talk.

NOTE: The topic of affirmations is too broad to cover in this book. However, there are many excellent books on this topic you can use to help develop your own set of daily affirmations.

7. *Use visualization to envision the success you desire.*

   Visualizing your success ahead of time will enable your subconscious mind to begin to believe it can – and will – really happen. The more fully you can engage all your senses in the visualization, the better. Again, this topic is too deep to adequately cover here, but there are many excellent books written on this topic, as well.

8. *Include the other person in your new plans. Allow them to help you plan the changes, as well as implement them.*

   Excluding a significant other from your new plans is a devastating step to take. It makes that person feel as though you don't care about him and his opinions, and that you're going to do what you want to do no matter how he feels about it – and now won't consult him for advice, nor will you give him the consideration due him as part of the family. By gaining buy-in from that person, you can develop a plan together that includes tolerance in the short-term and success in the long-term for everyone, not just for one person.

9. *Give it time.*

These changes will take time. Don't go into this process with the unrealistic expectation that all you have to do is talk about it once and everything will magically change. Some of these beliefs have been held for 20, 30, 40 years – or more. They will not change overnight! You'll probably take two steps forward and one step back – or one step forward and two steps back at first. Give the process – and the other person – the time needed to adjust to the changes, begin to break old habits and discover new ways of interacting with you.

10. *Make a decision – and act on it.*

Don't give up in your attempt to achieve your dreams, whether it will occur within the current relationship or outside of it. There may be ways for you to reach your dreams while not involving the other person, allowing him to "do his thing" while you do yours. However, if this is not possible and all else fails in the relationship, it may be time to take a good hard look at it and determine if it's ever going to work for you – or for the other person. If not, it may be time to rectify the situation, get out of that relationship and find one that will be more rewarding to all parties. While I'm not encouraging people to throw away long-term or good relationships that just need some work, I do believe that there are destructive relationships that do neither party any good and that should be dissolved. Only you can determine into which category your difficult relationship falls.

Overview

Myths to bust:

Myth #1:

I must be Superwoman to have a career outside the home and have children, a husband and a well-run home. I must do it all myself, without help from others.

Myth #2:

Women are just "playing around" in their careers; men are the *real* breadwinners of the family

Myth #3:

A woman who spends money to launch a business career is taking food out of her children's mouths and money out of her family's pocket.

Myth #4:

Women who make more money than their husbands are "showing them up"

Myth #5:

Women should be happy just taking care of their husbands and children, even after the children are grown. They shouldn't need other outside interests.

Myths to bust continued:

Myth #6:

Women should put their families above any other personal and professional goals, which do not have an appropriate place in a woman's life.

Myth #7:

The goals of women who want to stay home to raise their children and care for their families are not as worthwhile as those of women who desire a career outside the home.

What myths do I buy into?

____

____

How can I bust them?

____

____

Most common excuses we use to justify our fears and inactivity:

- I have to do everything myself – there's no one who can help me
- If you want something done right, you have to do it yourself!
- No one can do it as well as I can
- It will take longer to show someone else how to do it than to do it myself
- I have no marketable skills
- I've been out of the workforce for too long/I've never held a job outside the home
- I don't have enough time

My "favorite" excuses used to justify my fears and inactivity:

Tips to overcome fear and take action:

1. Recognize limiting attitudes and beliefs do exist.
2. Talk to the other person about the fact that he or she seems to promote one or more of these attitudes.
3. Gain a commitment from the other person to change these beliefs, as well as her actions toward you.
4. If you can't get the other person to accept your opinions and at least attempt to change, seek professional help.
5. Stop the negative self-talk. Seek professional help, if necessary.
6. Recite positive affirmations that reinforce the beliefs you wish to hold.
7. Use visualization to envision the success you desire.
8. Include the other person in your new plans. Allow them to help you plan the changes, as well as implement them.
9. Give it time.
10. Make a decision – and act on it.

Part II:

Success Stories of Everyday Heroes

Chapter Eleven

Everyday Heroes

a.k.a. Success Stories

One important thing I've noticed about many great success stories of our time is that they often involve people who have changed their lives and achieved greatness despite (and sometimes due to) tragic events in their lives. These are truly heroic stories, and we do need to hear them.

However, millions of us have never experienced (and hopefully will never endure) cataclysmic events of such proportions. Consequently, while these stories are inspiring, many of us cannot completely relate to them. Most often, it's simply because we don't believe ourselves capable of such courage. Even though we *may* possess courage of this magnitude, most of us will thankfully never know it.

Other success stories involve those who have achieved great fame, public stature or financial wealth. Again, while they inspire and awe us, many of us do not have the same aspirations, nor can we fully relate to those who do.

What we *can* relate to are stories of people "just like us", who have led quiet but inspiring and successful lives. However, simply because they're not "newsworthy" we don't often hear about those whose successes are not caused by spectacular events. Their stories are out there, and we need to look for them all around us, pay attention to them and allow them to give us inspiration so they impact our own lives in a positive way.

I know first-hand the impact that everyday success stories can have in inspiring others because it happened to me. I had always believed that I would be successful in my professional life, but had subconsciously placed a limit on *how* successful I would be, not to mention in which field I would obtain professional success. Certainly, I never dreamed I would earn a high income, nor would I ever be in a high position in any company - and I held myself (and my income) down due to this belief. However, when I began to see examples of others, ordinary men and women *just like me* earning high incomes and great success *in my chosen career*, the seeds of the belief that "if they could do it, I could do it" were sown. Once I saw examples I could relate to, I began to believe I could do it, too. This was the key to turning my career around and allowing me to believe in, and then create, my own success.

I had always believed I would be successful in my personal life, as well. However, even though I love my personal life as it has turned out, life had different plans for me than the ones I thought would transpire. I had always dreamed of having children of my own, but my body had other plans and refused to cooperate. When we discovered that I couldn't have children, it seemed a devastating blow.

But I looked around me at other people who had experienced the same thing I had and realized that this was not the only defining event in one's life. Other people had made great successes of their lives, with and without children of their own. I saw their successes and realized that if children were not in the plan for me, I would find a way to be fulfilled through other means. After all, I already had a great start in my loving husband and his two children. I was blessed to have them, and determined to make our life together happy. I now enjoy a loving relationship with all of them, and my happiness has been compounded with the addition of grandchildren! I'm now known as "Nana", a title as special as I had always dreamed it would be. And thanks to a very special woman in Japan, who came to live with us for a year as an exchange student, I have known the pleasure of being called "Mom." I continue to be thankful that I didn't give up on attaining my own happiness, simply because of a setback over which I had no control.

It is through the success stories of other ordinary people that we see how we too can achieve our own success. By their examples, we believe success is possible and aspire to it in our own lives. Through these examples and the lessons they teach, we learn what persistence and determination can do for all of us, including those of us who have never been tragically affected by one singularly devastating event in our lives, but who must overcome our own obstacles every day nonetheless.

The following is a list of the lessons I've learned from the stories of the people in this chapter. While all of the stories demonstrate each lesson in one way or another, I've indicated the story I believe most illuminates that lesson. They are lessons you can not only employ in your own life, but use to instill hope in your children at an early age, as well as a sense of purpose and a feeling of self-respect, dignity and pride. These stories also demonstrate the future benefits of positive actions taken early – and often - in life, as well as the impact of corrective actions taken at appropriate times as we live and grow.

By the way, every one of the individuals in the stories contained in this chapter expressed the fact that they felt honored and flattered (some even expressed surprise) by my request for permission to include them in this book. Because we've all been so conditioned to believe that only those who have achieved great wealth, great stature or great fame can inspire others, some found it hard to believe their stories would inspire those who read the book. What I know is that each and every one of us is an inspiration to someone, and each of these people's stories were inspirations to me in ways they cannot begin to realize.

Because of this, I dedicate this chapter to the quiet heroes and sheroes in our lives who guide us with their values, teach us with their actions and inspire us with their strength, and to the individuals who bring those values to life and whose stories are contained herein. I hope you enjoy them as much as I did.

Lesson #	*Lesson Learned*	*Best Illustrated By*
Lesson #1:	Faith in a higher power will guide you to a higher purpose and give you strength of character and the will to continue, even in the face of obstacles.	Cora Miles-Jefferson
Lesson #2:	A clear vision of where you are going will help you succeed at achieving a goal, even when it's extremely complex and/or long-term.	Kenneth Johnson
Lesson #3:	If you don't ask for what you want, you will never get it. You must let others know what you want to do, keep trying and asking – and never give up! It may take a while, but you will reach your goal.	Bruce Geroux
Lesson #4:	Just because no one's ever done something before doesn't mean it can't be done. Follow your dreams – no matter where they take you. You may even pave the way for others.	Ann Brown Payne

Lesson #5:	You can always find plenty of people who will tell you that what you want to do is impossible. But if you're persistent and creative enough to think differently, and if the goal is important enough to you, you will find a way.	Jean Smith
Lesson #6:	Don't take NO for an answer. If you know in your heart that what you're doing is right for you, keep going! Find another way. And if you find yourself on a path that leads away from your dream, change course and get back on the right path. If you do this, you will find your dream.	Jana Stanfield
Lesson #7:	It doesn't matter where you started in life or in business…if you continue to improve yourself and believe in what you want to achieve, you will do it.	Everyone

The Lord's Purpose

Born in a small town in Georgia, Cora Miles-Jefferson knows what it's like to focus on a dream and pursue it from an early age. Cora always believed she could be somebody, a belief instilled in her by her mom, Irene Adams, a short little lady with a big heart and strong values who has always been a big influence in Cora's life and her pursuit of excellence. She always taught Cora that what matters most is not *what* you do, but *how* you do it.

During Cora's early life, whenever she tried to find an excuse not to go out in the hot sun and pick beans with the rest of her family, her mom and sisters thought she was lazy. But Cora wasn't lazy; she has always believed in working for what she wanted. She dreamed of what she wanted at an early age – and it wasn't to be laboring in the hot sun, but in an office with air conditioning, running businesses and wearing business suits that reflect success.

While growing up, Cora carefully observed people from the corporate world. She noticed the way they carried themselves and the way they dressed, and she set her sights on becoming a part of that world. *Dress for Success* was the motto she always kept in mind. By identifying early on with people whose destinies she admired and wanted to be like, she remained focused on her dream of being part of that culture.

Even though Cora wanted a career, she began a family at a very young age, marrying at age 16 and having her first child at age 17. She and her husband moved to Daytona, Florida for employment reasons, placing Cora far away from her family for the first time in her life.

Cora threw herself into her new family and also enrolled at Daytona Community College. While there, she took business classes, at one point filling out an Interest Assessment on which she indicated a desire to be a bank teller, a simple act that would lead to a long and successful career in the financial industry. Shortly after Cora filled out that Assessment, a representative from Security First National Bank came to the college and asked if anyone in her class wanted to be a bank teller. Cora raised her hand and she was hired!

Once there, Cora's inquisitive nature caused her to seek answers to questions behind the scenes, constantly inquiring about the inner workings of the bank. In addition to her duties as a teller, she learned how to perform other functions. Her diligent nature and commitment to doing the best job possible enabled her to quickly work her way up to higher positions. After one year, she entered training as a New Accounts Representative, acquiring that position the next year.

As fate would have it, while Cora's career was progressing, her home life was not. After five years and two children, she and her husband divorced. She left Daytona and moved to Orlando, where she had to start all over again – as a bank teller at Great Western Bank. It broke Cora's heart to start back at the bottom, but her heart was in banking. She also had two boys to support. These two facts kept her going. Not able to make ends meet on a teller's salary, she was forced to work two or three jobs to support her family, something Cora took very seriously.

While at Great Western, Cora mingled with senior industry executives at the traditional wine-and-cheese parties, where she was often the only

African-American attendee. Some of her co-workers told her not to go because they felt she was a "token", but Cora realized it wasn't about that. She wanted to associate with the powerful and successful people she wanted to be like. She didn't care if she (or they) were African-American or not; "token" or not, she would do what benefited herself as well as the bank and wouldn't let that kind of negative thinking stop her. She also joined the Urban Bankers Association, where she met Ann Brown Payne.

Once again, Cora's commitment to excellence and her philosophy that "you never know who's watching you and how you present yourself – so be your best at all times" had paid off. She made quite an impression on Ann, influencing Ann to mentor and encourage her. When Ann took over as President of Metro Savings Bank, she hired Cora. Once there Cora shone, working her way up to Vice President within two years!

Later, when Ann moved to the Minority/Women Business Enterprise Alliance in Orlando, Florida, she asked Cora to join her in assisting minority- and women-owned business owners with starting up their businesses, furthering their careers and contributing to the community. Cora served in the capacity of Vice President at the Alliance, a job she loved and in which she truly felt she was doing God's work for her community.

Cora believes God plants people like seeds in your life, to help you believe in yourself and achieve more. Throughout her life, Cora has recognized these "seeds" and is thankful for the role they've played. Ann was one of them. During a prior job at the Daytona Police Department, a man named Sgt. Shaw was another. While at times he pushed Cora to her limits, she respected him and knew he would not do so if he didn't believe she was capable of doing more. Sgt. Shaw may not realize the impact he made on her belief in herself to make it through tough times, but Cora does – and the impact is unmistakable.

Although her work at the Alliance was very rewarding for Cora, it was not the final career for her. Through a ministry at their church, one of her sons had begun to perform with other boys his age in a group called the Mime Boys. They paint their faces white and mime to spiritual songs, now giving tremendously successful and inspiring performances throughout the country at spiritual and youth gatherings.

This gave rise to a long-hidden dream of Cora's to start a talent management company. Cora's plan is to eventually move into full-time talent management. She has already opened the doors of her own company, Diamante Management Services (the name is a combination of her two sons' names), where she currently manages and guides young artists' careers.

Due to her commitment to quality, her pride in herself and how she represents the organizations she chooses to be a part of, and her constant quest for self-improvement, Cora has been a vital and senior part of every organization she has joined. She has helped others achieve their own success and is now guiding even more in the pursuit of their own dreams.

Cora attributes this success throughout her adult life to three main factors:

1) Persistence and focus. Cora knew she had to support herself and her two boys; she needed a job and had to keep her eye on her goal, repeating to herself, "There is something on the other side of 'through' (gesturing breaking through a wall) and I'm going to make it, even though it isn't easy!"
2) Pride in herself and her work. Whatever position she held, Cora *always* put her best foot forward, causing others to notice her and want her to be part of their management teams.
3) Her faith in God. Cora's strong faith in God has played a major role in her success throughout her life. She believes God has

great plans for her, and she is determined not to quit on those plans.

From youngster working in the fields of Georgia, to young mother, to bank teller, to bank Vice President, to Alliance Vice President, to talent management, Cora has made her mark and inspired others' belief in her throughout her entire life.

One thing Cora knows for certain: she loves what she is doing, and she looks forward to whatever the Lord has in store for her next!

Through the Eyes of a Soldier

On April 26, 1994, Kenneth Johnson realized a lifelong dream. He had become a member of the 3rd U.S. Infantry, known as the Old Guard, the official military unit whose members are specially selected to serve the President of the United States as his Presidential Honor Guard for all military and formal ceremonies in Washington, DC. On that day, this elite corps of soldiers accompanied former President Richard M. Nixon's casket from Washington, DC to El Toro Marine Air Station and through the streets of Yorba Linda, California as the motorcade made its way toward his final resting place in the gardens of the Richard Nixon Library & Birthplace. These dignified soldiers continued to stand guard over the President's casket until the State funeral began the next day, closing a 40-year chapter that resulted in the proudest moment of Kenneth's life.

Kenneth remembers the exact moment his dream was born. It was during the four long days following President John F. Kennedy's assassination. As President Kennedy lay in state, and as his funeral procession slowly rolled along the streets of Washington, DC, 8-year-old Kenneth Johnson watched, mesmerized, as the events unfolded on his family's television set in Orlando, Florida, far away from the actual scene but just as real to him as if he had been right there beside those men in Washington. However, young Kenneth's interest lay not in the President himself, but in the soldiers who accompanied the President on his final journey.

He was captivated by the way they conducted themselves, how they moved with precision during the changing of the guard, how they carried themselves and how they lent a solemn dignity to the entire proceeding. He noticed the color of their uniforms, their style, and their demeanor. And he knew that was what he wanted to be someday. He wanted to be one of the men who accompanied the President on the most solemn and final event of his Presidency – and his life.

From that time on, Kenneth's thoughts and dreams were consumed by this desire. He played "soldier" with his friends – not just the "bang! bang!" kind of soldiering common to most children. Kenneth played the "elite" soldier, standing straight and proud, marching, saluting, and practicing spinning his "rifle". He was always clear about exactly what kind of soldier he wanted to be. He had seen the image on television and kept that image clearly in his mind.

This image, and the vision of himself as one of those soldiers, kept Kenneth out of serious trouble throughout his teen years. This is not to say he was a perfect child; in fact, like most teenage boys, he had a rather wild side and a strong will that got him into occasional trouble. But early on his mother and father had instilled in him and his nine brothers and sisters a strong sense of family values and a healthy self-respect that kept him from making serious mistakes that would have jeopardized his chances of reaching his goals later on in life. His mother, who knew of his dream to be in the Honor Guard, also took an active part in his education, insisting that schoolwork be done before he could go out and play, keeping Kenneth focused on getting good grades in school and helping him realize that this was essential if he wanted to reach his ultimate goal. His father was also a strong disciplinarian, and whenever Kenneth "tested" his father, he usually regretted his misdeeds because the consequences of his actions were swift.

Although Kenneth didn't write down his goals when he was young, in the traditional way we usually envision writing goals, he did have an artistic side, a talent he inherited from his father. Instead of writing his goals in cursive, Kenneth did what came naturally to him, drawing military-type pictures depicting his goals, which served to keep him focused on them.

Kenneth's plan was to join the military and begin working immediately on becoming part of the elite group he'd seen on television. However, fate had other plans and in 1970, at age 18, he was drafted and sent to Viet Nam, where he served his country for eight months. Kenneth feels that one of the most crucial factors in his survival during those long and difficult months was the strong conviction that he could do whatever he wanted to do if he put his mind to it, a conviction instilled in him by his mother. He also kept a journal, beginning with his first day in Viet Nam, an exercise that helped him deal with this part of his life as it occurred.

When Kenneth finished his tour of duty in Viet Nam, he was stationed in Europe, where he began to work in earnest on his plan to achieve his dream of being a member of the Old Guard. He researched that "type" of soldier and asked his supervisors what he should do to get into that unit. They told him he needed to "be the best soldier there was" because only the best of the best are chosen. They explained to Kenneth that he could not apply to be in that unit – the only way into it was to be selected, a privilege that required a lot of effort, achievement and hard work.

Kenneth started to work on this right away. Whenever he met a member of the Old Guard, he immediately noticed that they looked different, they walked differently, their uniforms were noticeably neater. He constantly grilled them, asking them to mentor him and teach him how to stand correctly, how to do a proper about-face and rifle spin; he even questioned them about their posture. With their guidance, and working from illustrations in military books, he practiced diligently in an effort to perfect his image and his form.

Kenneth began to maintain his uniform better than the average soldier. He always did his job to the very best of his ability, and volunteered for jobs others didn't want to do, in an effort to get noticed for excellence in his field. Each time he did so, he was rewarded with a higher rank and more responsibility. Kenneth would go on to become one of the youngest members of the military to go from Private (rank E-1) to Sergeant 1st Class (rank E-7), achieving this rank in an unbelievable seven years, a feat which usually takes 10 years or longer to accomplish.

Preparing himself mentally so he was ready when the opportunity presented itself was also key for Kenneth. He repeatedly told himself, "I can do this." Because of his keen interest in the event that had inspired his dream, Kenneth had bought the book "Four Days", which not only chronicled the four days following President Kennedy's assassination, but inspired Kenneth and helped him keep his dream alive. He bought military instruction books and used all these books not only to motivate and teach himself, but to teach the men under his command as well.

He also decided to appear before various Boards, winning each one as he tried for it: Soldier of the Quarter, Soldier of the Month, NCO of the Quarter and NCO of the Month. While serving in Germany, Kenneth's superior officer, Sgt. Major James, approached him and suggested he try to become a member of the Sergeant Morales Club, a group that represents the highest overseas honor a soldier can receive.

This is the point at which Kenneth's resolve was tested the most. Being human and becoming weary from years of effort striving for perfection, Kenneth initially refused, claiming that membership in this group was too tough and that he didn't want to study *that* hard. At this time, Kenneth had no idea of the impact that membership in this club would make on his future goal to become a member of the Old Guard. Sgt. Major James looked at Kenneth when he refused to try for it and replied, "Good, being a Sgt. 1st Class, you probably won't make it anyway."

That comment was all Kenneth needed to spur him into action. One thing you must know if you are to understand Kenneth Johnson is that, when challenged he will work endlessly to succeed in overcoming that challenge. By telling him he probably wouldn't make it, Sgt. Major James had issued a major challenge to Kenneth – one that he simply couldn't ignore. Kenneth knows in his heart that Sgt. Major James said this to him intentionally, knowing it would spur him to accomplish this goal. He was right.

Kenneth threw himself back into his studies and when he felt he was prepared, he went before the First Board review and made it through; then he tackled the Second Board and succeeded at that one. Finally, he was ready for the Third and final Board. Sgt. Major James accompanied him to this review, in which Kenneth was relentlessly drilled by eight other sergeant majors at the highest regimental level. An hour later, the newest member of the elite Sergeant Morales Club emerged and shook the hand of Sgt. Major James in a show of pride and gratitude for the motivation his superior officer had given him to achieve this honor.

When then-3-Star General and brother Mason Colin Powell pinned the Army Commendation Medal to Kenneth's shoulder in a formal ceremony honoring his entry into the Sergeant Morales Club, he leaned over and whispered in Kenneth's ear, "Brother, I'm proud of you."

Kenneth now knows that this honor was the final key, in a long record of exceptional effort and achievement, to his being selected for the Old Guard, where he served for six proud years, culminating with his participation in the Honor Guard upon President Nixon's death.

After 40 years, Kenneth Johnson had achieved a lifelong dream. Through hard work, persistence and focus, he was able to nurture and achieve this dream. But it's not all over for Kenneth. If you were to ask him what's next, he'd tell you he doesn't know exactly what will be next, but he can tell you this – he's not done yet!

The Long Journey

The door closed, and in that moment two-year-old Bruce's family life was forever altered. Bruce's father had walked out on his wife and six young children, leaving them with no father figure in their lives and very little financial support.

The year was 1942 and they lived in upstate New York. When Bruce's father left the family, his mother had difficulty making ends meet, working two or three jobs in an effort to keep her family clothed, fed and warm. She managed to keep them all together for four years, when she was notified by their landlord that their house was to be occupied by his son; they had to leave.

In 1946, no one would rent to a divorced woman with six children. Bruce's mother was forced to make the agonizing decision to split up her family, boarding five of her children with other families whom she paid to take them in. Her eldest son remained with her, while two sons went to live with a second family. Bruce and his younger twin sisters went to live with a third.

Because these families often couldn't keep the children long, the children frequently moved, alternating living with their grandparents until another family could be found. None of them knew how long they'd be in one place or how far they'd live from their mother and siblings, as they were shuffled from home to home and from school to school.

At one point, Bruce and his sisters were sent to a family living in a town five miles away. While not far by today's standards, Bruce's mother didn't own a car and had no way to visit them. She traveled to and from her jobs by bus, working long hours, and often not arriving home until midnight. At this point, Bruce and his sisters saw their mother only about once a month.

One of the families lived in a poverty-stricken area. While they had a typical but simple house, the family across the street had one made only of outside walls with studs on the inside. There was no money for insulation or wallboard to make interior walls, and there was no indoor plumbing; they had only an outhouse.

Bruce's "family" planted vegetables and fruits, which they picked and canned in the fall to last throughout the year. Their source of meat was whatever the father could hunt. If he was lucky, he shot a bear or deer. He also hunted pheasant, rabbit, squirrel, birds or whatever he could find; in addition, they raised chickens and pigs as often as they could afford it, freezing extra meat after the slaughter. Even so, there was often no meat and the evening meal consisted of a boiled potato covered with grease from a small piece of fried salt pork to give the potato a little flavor; if the canned vegetables lasted, they added a little vegetable or some relish to the plate with the potato. Bruce remembers eating ketchup sandwiches because there was nothing to put in the bread, as well as cereal with condensed milk because the milkman wouldn't deliver milk when the family got behind on their milk bill.

Sometimes they would run out of oil and didn't have money to buy more, leaving them without fuel to heat the house or cook their food. During those times, they collected as much scrap wood and kindling as they could find, since their propane kitchen stove had a small wood stove on the side. The wood stove created enough heat to bake in the oven or cook on a hotplate, as well as heat the kitchen, the one room that had heat during winters when temperatures often fell to 20° and 30° below zero and stayed there for weeks.

Despite this, Bruce considered himself fortunate because at least there was always *something* to eat, and he did have shoes year-round. The children across the street had no shoes in the summer because each got one pair of new shoes at the start of every school year, which had to last until the next one. By summer, the shoes were worn through and useless. The local grocery store donated old vegetables and fruits to this family, and often that's all they had to eat.

Although Bruce was a good boy, the lack of a stable family life took its toll on him. He failed kindergarten and had to repeat it. He passed every grade after that until 8th grade. During that year, two events happened that changed his attitude and the potential direction of his life.

The first was that he failed eighth grade. The second, and more devastating, was that he joined a couple of friends who had broken into a nearby home. While the other boys rummaged around, trying to find things to steal, Bruce found a shotgun and some bullets. Never having shot a gun before and curious about how it worked, he loaded the gun and began fiddling with the trigger and safety mechanisms trying to figure out how to shoot it. The gun went off and almost took his foot off when it did. Luckily, it missed by inches and the bullet blasted into the ground.

The noise attracted the attention of a neighbor, who called the police. Fortunately for Bruce, the other boys had lied and told him the home belonged to a friend of one of their fathers who had said they could go there whenever they wanted to; they repeated this to the police, preventing Bruce from being formally charged with breaking and entering.

However, when Bruce's mother arrived at the police station to take him home, he watched while she arranged for his release. At that moment,

Bruce felt worse than he had ever felt before, as he saw the look on her face. The story it told made a lasting impression, for it was filled with sadness and asked the question, "Where did *I* go wrong?" Bruce knew his mother was blaming herself for his misdeeds, and he vowed never to do anything again that would make his mother look and feel the way she did right then.

After this, Bruce's mother brought him home to live with her. She had remarried and her new husband had just completed building additional rooms onto his home for her children. The family was reunited and Bruce's mother was able to keep a close eye on him from that point on.

Bruce didn't know what he wanted to do for a career, but during his senior year of high school he took accounting and bookkeeping and discovered he was good at it. However, having chosen the Business rather than the College curriculum, he also discovered he hadn't taken the proper courses to enter college. He consulted his guidance counselor, who told him it was too late to change his mind and dismissed Bruce, but pointed to a bookcase, saying, "There are a bunch of college books over there; maybe you can find someone who will take you, but I doubt it." Undaunted, Bruce searched through the catalogs and found a two-year college that would accept him – and it offered an Accounting degree! He finished high school in 1960 and entered Cobleskill Agricultural College in Cobleskill, NY.

After graduating in 1962 and experiencing difficulty finding an accounting job, Bruce entered the workforce in a retail store as part of their management trainee program. While there, he discovered he hated the position he was in, but absolutely loved the machines in the office – the calculators and the "data processing" machines - and he longed to learn how to program them. His dream of becoming a programmer had been born.

However, in 1963 Bruce received a military draft notice and, not wanting to be forced into the Army, he signed up for the Air Force since he heard they offered training and would pay for his education. He expressed his desire for data processing training to his superior officers, but they refused to train him in this right away. He was assigned as a supply specialist. The closest he got to the computers was being able to look in at them through the windows of the computer room.

He asked his superior officers over and over to transfer him, pointing to the computer room and saying, "I want to work in there; please let me work in there." Finally, due to his persistence, he was transferred into the computer room as a computer operator. He had taken his first step toward being a programmer – working with the actual machines!

Soon he was notified he was being transferred to Alaska. He requested a computer room position; request denied – the computer room was out of his group's jurisdiction. Shortly after arrival, however, he discovered his group was about to get a new computer and train several men for computer operations positions to run it. Bruce asked to be included, but they had already chosen five men of senior rank and couldn't afford to send another.

Again undaunted, Bruce asked what the problem was. He was told there wasn't enough money for the flight to Texas to attend the school. Bruce offered to pay for the flight himself, which impressed his superior officer so much he said, "If you want to go *that* badly, we'll send you." They paid for his flight and Bruce was trained with the rest of the men.

Upon completing four years in the Air Force, Bruce found a job as a computer operator at a large retail company, hoping to work his way up to programmer as soon as possible. While there, he enrolled at Northeastern University, taking night courses to earn his Bachelor degree in Business Management, a degree that included a programming course.

This course helped lay the groundwork for Bruce's later advancement into his chosen field.

Bruce worked hard and gained promotion after promotion. He began as a 3rd shift operator, moving to supervisor, then moving up the ranks to 2nd shift and then to 1st shift supervisor. All along the way, he told his managers he wanted to be a programmer. After six years of proving himself and asking for a programming position, they finally gave him one, helping him realize a dream he had worked toward for 10 years.

Bruce has been in programming and programming management ever since, and has loved every minute of the last 30 years spent in his dream career. As computers have changed and grown, so has he, updating his skills as needed. With the advent of powerful personal computers, Bruce has changed gears again. He has discovered the world of personal computers, websites and programs to work with those sites, and loves the work he currently does on them.

Bruce's story shows us how you can achieve your dream, no matter where begin, if you persist, commit to a goal and take action. One other point is very important to note: if Bruce hadn't kept letting others in higher positions know of his desire to move into his desired career, if he hadn't been willing to invest in himself, and if he hadn't proven he was worth being given a chance, his dream never would have been accomplished.

If it hadn't been for these factors, who knows where Bruce would be now or what unsatisfying jobs he may have held during the last 30 years. But I'm very happy for him, and for myself, that he accomplished his dream – because this is the story of Bruce Geroux, a man I have been proud and honored for the past 23+ years to call my husband.

Encouragement from "The Rock"

She was born Ann Brown, the youngest of five children. Her mother wanted her to be a teacher because teachers were polished and revered, they held status in the community and there was a sincere respect for education at that time. She almost cried when Ann told her she would not become a teacher, opting instead to enter the world of business.

Viewing attendance at college as her first career eliminated the question of whether or not to enroll. Ann had to do *something* once she graduated from high school, and since she didn't know exactly what to do, she attended college to help her decide, enrolling at Florida A&M. Once there, she began to research various occupations. Every time she came upon another good possibility, she changed her major to accommodate that career, changing it three times during the first week!

Through her research, Ann began to notice a difference between the salaries of teachers and those who worked in private business. Although this was not the only factor in her decision to enter the corporate world, it was one of them. Another factor was that business majors actually *carried* themselves differently, a visual difference Ann couldn't help but notice – and desire. She finally settled on a major in Business Administration, with minors in Accounting, Finance and Marketing.

Ann did not start out with aspirations to own her own business. However, in college she began a business as a seamstress without realizing she had done exactly that. She began sewing for six families and made costumes for May Day, moving on to making band uniforms for the school. Before she knew it, she was a business owner with many clients!

In 1977, after only 3+ years, Ann graduated, becoming the first member of her family to earn a college degree.

Job offers came from Connecticut, New York, Tampa and Atlanta. But fear set in and Ann, not wanting to leave home, turned down many lucrative offers. She accepted an offer from a local non-profit organization, becoming Executive Assistant for the Executive Director of Human Resources Clearing House. In this position, she dealt with community service issues: youth employment, Big Brothers and Sisters, summer tutorial programs and CETA, a workforce development program, acquiring much responsibility in a very short time.

After just three months, she was promoted to Fiscal Officer and Program Manager, accepting responsibility for financial administration, grant-writing and program management. In this role, she also taught non-profit organizations how to manage grants and make presentations to professional fundraisers.

She remained in this position for two years, at which time Ann decided she wanted to work for a large corporation. In 1979, although fearful of what lay ahead as well as leaving her comfortable position behind, she packed up, drove a U-Haul to Orlando, returned to Florida A&M School of Business as an alumna, and began interviewing with Fortune 500 companies, being hired within four months for a position as a management trainee at Sun Bank, N.A.

In this position, she was in unfamiliar territory since there had been only two African-American employees before her. In fact, an African-American colleague told her it would be impossible for her to become an officer due to her race. Although Ann had used other excuses to hold herself back at times, she never gave *that* excuse any power over her. True to form, and remembering her grandmother's words that she would only be limited by herself, Ann refused to accept this stereotype, putting her race aside and going for it. She found a mentor in the "toughest guy" in the Sun Bank system; she also volunteered often, knowing this was a way for others to get to know who she was. Due to hard work and perseverance, she became an officer within 8 months, a process that normally took two years!

While at the bank, Ann studied annual reports and noticed a trend in which revenue-generating positions were revered while others such as human relations and community affairs, although important, were often cut. She decided to move into Community Lending, forcing herself to make the difficult decision to go through the management trainee program a second time in order to accomplish this goal. It worked, and Ann remained at the bank until 1995, holding 12-14 positions and ending her tenure in the position of Vice President and Operations Officer.

Ann had received many other job offers while working at Sun Bank, but fear (among other things) stopped her from accepting them. Like many of us, Ann used excuses to justify her fears, including "It's a big responsibility," or "If I do that, I'll need to move again."

However, the right offer came along at a time when Ann was ready to accept it, and in 1995 Ann accepted the position of President and CEO of Metro Savings Bank in Orlando, FL, becoming the first African-American to become President of any Florida bank, as well as the first female President of Metro.

This was a very challenging time for Ann. She worked 70-80 hours per week, trying to effect changes while encountering resistance, struggling to help this community bank thrive.

At the same time, Ann also owned a store whose employees were stealing from her. On the personal side, Ann's life was also suffering as she and her husband divorced in addition to her recent encounters with personal jealousy from others due to her career and position in the community. The combined strain threatened burnout and caused her to gain 40 pounds as she fought to win the battle to remain focused on her goals and deal with the distractions in her way.

By persevering, she finally did win these battles. After two years of effort the bank was thriving, her divorce was over and she had sold the store. She attributes these accomplishments to her passion, focus and mission, as well as having an excellent management team at the bank to help her execute that mission. She firmly believes everyone must have a mission and a good support system to succeed, whether it's in business, in marriage or in life.

This two-year "trial by fire" prepared her for her work at the Minority/Woman Business Enterprise Alliance. She worked closely with the Mayor's office to write its job descriptions, mission and vision. In 1997, the Alliance opened with Ann as its President, helping minority- and women-owned businesses start up and grow. Ann needed a strong commitment for this effort as well, since she had to help those who didn't like the changes she was making understand the vital nature of this contribution to the community.

Throughout these experiences, Ann has learned some valuable lessons she'd like to share. The first is to find a mentor to help you achieve your goals. Ann has had several throughout her life, the greatest being her grandmother, nicknamed "The Rock", who imparted much wisdom and encouragement early on. She also took inspiration from Nelson Mandela, whose words inspired her not to worry about what others say, but to do what was right and focus on her goals.

She also has an important insight to share with career-focused individuals, men and women alike. While her early focus was to earn money and build her career, it has now shifted to other priorities: quality of life, family, spiritual matters, and mental and emotional well-being. She does not want to be a slave to money; she wants it to be the other way around.

Ann also has a message for aspiring and current female executives. Ann sees the two biggest challenges facing these women as 1) delegating, and 2) saying "no" when necessary. She notices a difference in attitude from others when they deal with her as a CEO. Whenever a male CEO is unavailable or unable to help, this fact is accepted without question. However, as a female CEO, she is often expected to try to do *something* anyway. She attributes this phenomenon to women's nurturing nature and knows women must fight hard to maintain balance in their lives and careers due to this perceived, but false, obligation to do too much.

Another piece of advice Ann offers is this: whenever she becomes fearful about what is happening in her life or her business, she conquers it with her faith and trust in God. She puts the matter into His hands, and allows the solution to come from His inspiration and guidance. She offsets her fears with focus, planning, prayer and execution, which help her accomplish all she sets out to do, even against immeasurable odds.

Although Ann's greatest compliment to date came from the business world in the year 2002, when someone she had helped start a business told her she had helped him make millions of dollars, she still has aspirations to be a college professor, something she attributes to her family's early love and respect for education. But first, she has important work to finish at the Alliance. She also has a further passion to help women. She envisions establishing a future women's group dedicated to mentoring women to succeed in business and in all aspects of life.

No matter what she does, I'm sure Ann's mother and grandmother are very proud of her accomplishments and will always be there for her in spirit, along with God, to guide her through the next challenge.

There Must Be A Way!

On a bitter cold evening in late January, 1999, Jean Smith* heard a knock on her door and opened it to find a sheriff standing on the porch of her home in Rehoboth, Massachusetts. The sheriff was there to serve her with a subpoena demanding that she go to court to explain why she hadn't refinanced or sold her home in order to remove her ex-husband's name from the mortgage and deed, as well as pay him $18,000 in equity owed to him. The deadline had been set for January 31, 1999. She broke down and cried...

Jean was born in 1956 in Seekonk, Massachusetts and married in January, 1978, creating what she believed would be a lifetime union. She and her husband lived in rented property for the first two years of their marriage. In 1980, they bought a modest home in East Providence, Rhode Island, where they stayed until they built their dream home in Rehoboth, Massachusetts in 1988.

Jean and her husband designed this home themselves, with Jean often working at an architect's table with pencil and t-square in hand, drawing out the layout as she envisioned it. The home was to occupy a piece of land they had bought in 1981. The land was out in the country and bordered a small pond Jean had fished upon as a child and that brought back many happy childhood memories. It was truly a dream house, in a dream location.

---

*Not Jean's real last name.

Jean and her family, which had now expanded to include three children, moved into their new home with high hopes in November, 1988, five days before Thanksgiving. She should have recognized the first clue that all was not well when she returned home from work that night to find that her husband had opened a celebratory bottle of champagne without waiting for her to get home.

Unfortunately, Jean missed these – and many other vital clues – for the next eight years, until their marital problems finally culminated in her returning home from work one night in May, 1996 to a husband who told her that he was unhappy, he was leaving, and that he already had another place to live. He had set the wheels for their separation in motion the week before, without telling her of his plans.

Jean was devastated, not to mention taken completely by surprise. Even though she had known there were issues they needed to resolve, she'd had no idea they were headed for divorce. However, she had no choice but to go through the motions, try to keep the rest of her family together and remain in the family home. Things were not to be easy for her.

In December of that year, after promising to make the mortgage payments on their home, Jean's husband decided not to pay the mortgage without telling her. In addition, he cancelled all of her credit cards (which were also in his name) without telling her. She discovered that her credit cards were no longer active when she tried to use them; she discovered that the December mortgage payment had not been made only when she attended an arbitration session for the divorce on December 5.

To add to Jean's distress, at the arbitration meeting, Jean's husband took half of the savings in an account with Jean's name on it. After the separation, Jean and one of her daughters had begun to save money together from their jobs, knowing that things would be tight and the money might be needed for a rainy day. They deposited their savings into an account with Jean's name on it, not feeling the need to open a separate account for their daughter's funds. At the arbitration, Jean's husband claimed the money as a "marital asset", even though none of it had been earned or saved during the marriage – and half of it actually belonged to his daughter. However, Jean was forced to write a check to him for half of the money right then and there, or they would have frozen her account, which represented all the money Jean could access for living expenses.

After that meeting, Jean's husband paid the December mortgage, but it was decided that Jean was to assume responsibility for future mortgage payments beginning in January, 1997.

At this time, her husband claimed that his business was virtually worthless, so Jean was to receive no alimony. Her husband was ordered to pay $235 per week in child support for the three children. The mortgage payments on the house equaled the total amount Jean made at her music director's job *before taxes.* This meant that she and her children would have to live on the child support payments alone, as well as whatever she and the children could make at other jobs in the meantime. Jean was determined to remain in her home because to lose her dream home in addition to everything else she had lost was so psychologically distressing to her that she could not even consider it. She was determined to find a way to make ends meet.

Jean did it. She managed to pay all her bills, scrimped where she could and even occasionally borrowed money from close friends to make ends meet. Her mother often helped out by buying and cooking food and bringing it to them. Jean's youngest daughter qualified for reduced-cost lunches at school, which helped. Jean even tried to get food stamps, but she was *just* over the guidelines and did not qualify.

Jean felt that at this time she was living "in a fog", just getting through the days, not sure she even realized how bad things were, which may have been a blessing at the time. However, things were about to go from bad to worse.

When her divorce decree came through, it included an order for her to refinance her home in order to remove her ex-husband's name from the mortgage note and deed, and also to pay him $18,000 in home equity due to him. Jean was willing to refinance the home to achieve these goals, and there was enough equity built up by that time to do it.

Jean went to her bank to refinance the loan. She was denied. She was confused; she had kept all her accounts current, and had incurred no debt, since all of the credit cards she had used in her marriage had been cancelled by her husband months before. Jean thought that maybe that bank was just being overly cautious. So she tried another bank, and another, and another – until she had tried 18 different banks, including the one that held her original mortgage. She was denied at all of them!

Jean did not discover the reason for these denials until she finally called a banker she had previously used for business. When she inquired as to the reason for the denials, he revealed a startling fact – one her own lawyer had not uncovered during her divorce proceedings. Unbeknownst to Jean, her ex-husband had incurred $30,000 of credit card debts on credit cards (for which Jean had no physical cards) that included her name as well as his, causing this balance to show up on her credit reports, which in turn caused the banks to refuse to allow her to refinance because "her" debt was too high. Since Jean's husband had paid all the bills during their marriage, she was not aware of these balances.

Had her lawyer discovered this fact before the divorce decree was final, it could have been taken care of in the final decree. Now Jean had to contend with removing this debt before she could refinance her home and fulfill her obligations under the final divorce decree.

Jean began to go through pages and pages of credit cards appearing under her name on her credit report, explaining the situation and requesting that they remove her name from the card. Some complied, but most refused, claiming that since her ex-husband was the "authorized user" (the one who had obtained the card), they required *his* authorization before they would remove her name from the "joint" account. She was able to reduce the amount of the debt showing up under her name somewhat, but not enough to refinance.

Jean had to remove that debt from her credit reports, or the refinance would not happen. This was the only factor stopping her from refinancing and fully complying with the court's orders. She met with her ex-husband's lawyer to discuss this issue, explaining that the debts were not hers, to which he replied, "So, what's that to my client?" Her ex-husband, present at this meeting, refused to write to the credit card companies to authorize removal of her name. Apparently so intent upon making everything as difficult as possible for Jean, he was willing to go to the point of actually *causing* her to be unable to comply with the instructions of the divorce decree (to refinance the house, remove his name from the deed and title and pay him his equity), knowing this would eventually lead to her arrest for "contempt of court" if she couldn't find a way to comply.

Jean began calling more banks, becoming more and more desperate as the January 31, 1999 deadline approached. Time after time she was denied a loan. She tried everything with the banks. She even offered to borrow the money to pay her ex-husband's credit card debt and allow him to pay her back over time, interest-free. He refused. She asked him again to call the credit card company and authorize the removal of her name from the accounts. Again he refused.

What made these denials even more frustrating was that, due to the much lower interest rate at the time of the refinance as well as the lower principal balance on the loan than when the loan was first granted, her new mortgage payments would actually have been *lower* than her current payments! However, the banks claimed her debt ratio was too high, and that was all they were interested in. Even her own bank, to whom she had already been making higher *on time* payments on her own for two years, would not allow her to refinance.

Finally, as Jean continued working with one mortgage broker, she asked an important question that finally led to the solution of her problem. Her income was too low compared to her debt (inclusive of the $30,000). However, part of her allowable income, in addition to her wages, was child support. Wages are taken into consideration as a "gross amount", meaning that all other factors are accounted for with the knowledge that some of the wages will not make it to the household due to withholding taxes, etc. Jean made the point that her child support payments did not have any taxes taken out before they reached her household, and she asked why they should be treated the same way as wages. Her question: "Couldn't the bank take into consideration the fact that her child support was a "net amount", thus equivalent to a higher "gross" amount in comparable wages?"

The mortgage broker was stunned. He told her that had never been done before, but knowing how desperate her situation was, he was willing to ask the question. It worked!! The mortgage company was able to treat the child support income in a manner comparable to higher gross wages and include that figure in its calculations – and she just made it. She was approved for the refinance! Her closing was scheduled for February 1, 1999 - one day after the deadline date, but it was the earliest they could do it and she felt confident that this one day would be no problem. She was right. So…

… when the sheriff came to the door bearing a subpoena on that January night in 1999, Jean did break down and cry – but it wasn't from sadness; it was with relief, for she had weathered the storm, held up under pressures that would have destroyed a weaker person, and emerged triumphant. True, her closing was scheduled one day late, but it was still just in time to save her home, salvage her dignity and finally allow her to begin a new journey toward future happiness.

Jean's story shows us just how resilient and creative the human spirit can be when faced with a goal so important that failure is not an option. For Jean, losing her home would have been a devastating blow from which she may not have recovered.

By forcing herself to do what she needed to do, even if it meant she just "went through the motions in a haze" for a while, Jean was able to get through the most devastating events in her life and find a way to create future happiness and success.

Jean proved that with the help of supportive family and friends, the love of her children and dogged persistence drawn from the strength of her inner reserves when faced with obstacles, there really is a way…

Live, Love, Laugh

Jana Stanfield is an incredibly talented singer and songwriter, intent on bringing a message of hope, courage and belief to everyone she touches. Jana performs what she calls "Keynote Concerts", mainly for organizations dedicated to helping others, during which she performs songs of inspiration and shares her story in order to encourage others to follow their dreams, as she has followed hers.

The first time I saw Jana, she was performing a Keynote Concert for a National Speakers Association meeting. Her touching songs and personal story brought tears to my eyes as I recognized the truth in her words and its relation to many of my own struggles in the journey toward my dreams. She sang songs like *A Small Star*, which reminds us that "Even a small star shines in the darkness, for someone somewhere to see," and *If I Were Brave,* a song that asks the questions, "What would I do if I knew that I could not fail?" and "What would I do today if I were brave?"

Jana didn't just fall into success. Like most of us, she had to work hard at it, and even had to change direction a time or two before finding it. But she persisted and, as you will see from her story, it was all worth it.

Jana Stanfield was born in 1958 in Las Cruces, New Mexico to two musically-talented parents. Jana's father was a math teacher who started his first band in college and plays many instruments, sings and writes songs. Her mother, who was studying to be an elementary music teacher at the time of Jana's birth, plays piano and sings. Thus, Jana was immersed in music early on, literally cutting her teeth on the legs of her mom's Wurlitzer while her mother gave piano lessons in their home.

Throughout her early life, Jana's family would gather together as her mother played the piano and her father the guitar, while Jana and her brother and sister joined their parents in singing songs from the *Reader's Digest Family Songbook.*

Although her love of music never waned, Jana graduated from Eastern New Mexico University with a Radio & TV degree. During her junior and senior years of college, Jana enrolled in a two-year work/study program that required her to be in the field, shoot news stories, do editing back at the studio and then report the news on the air, actually doing a full news story every day in addition to her regular studies. Often, she couldn't find a cameraman to go on assignment with her, forcing her to act as her own cameraman. She would set the camera up on a tripod, focus it and then stand in front of it to record the story. When the story was captured, she often went back and edited the film herself. The necessity of performing multiple functions in order to produce the news gave her hands-on experience in all aspects of television news, as well as offering a tremendous opportunity to create demo videos, all of which she used to find a job after graduation.

You see, Jana naturally assumed she'd have to earn her own paycheck after graduation, a vision that differed quite sharply from many of her peers. When asked what they planned to do after graduation, many students said they would "Just move back in with my parents and see what happens." This was never an option for Jana! Because of her assumption that she would need a job, it became a goal for her to have one, to know where she was going and how she would pay her bills once out on her own. This goal was reinforced by her mother who gave her a powder-blue suit, and her grandmother who loaned her a white blouse. Jana bought herself a pair of black closed-toe low-heeled pumps to complete the outfit – her "interview suit" – which she wore to every job interview.

After sending her resume and demo videos everywhere during her senior year of college, Jana landed a job as a TV news reporter in Waco, TX immediately after graduation in 1982. She remained there for three months, when she was offered – and accepted – a much more prestigious position at an NBC station in Albuquerque, NM. The position also offered her a salary of $860 per month, a much higher salary than the $680 she was earning in Waco, sealing the deal.

Jana remained a television news reporter for four years. However, over the years, she had become increasingly disenchanted with this career, longing to become a singer. The question was how to do it. Every day she felt she was trapped in someone else's dream job, but had no idea how to transition into her own dream career. Feeling frustrated and immobilized by her lack of knowledge of what to do, she turned to her family. Her father knew the frustration she felt because he had felt it, too. He called Jana's uncle, Rev. Clyde Stanfield, a United Methodist minister and professional counselor, who took her out to lunch once a week to boost her spirits and offer whatever guidance he could. During one of these lunches, he taught her a process called "Three Steps, No Failure" that transformed her life.

Uncle Clyde told Jana she needed to build a bridge from where she was to where she wanted to go. The way to build this bridge was to select three activities she would accomplish during the next week *at which she could not possibly fail.* He explained that it was critical to select three things she was absolutely convinced she could do, to establish a track record of success right from the start. What was on Jana's first list?

1. Buy a book about making it in the music business
2. Call a voice teacher to see how much lessons would cost
3. Order cable television so she could watch The Nashville Network

For Jana, the beauty of this goal-setting method was that she didn't have to know exactly where she was going right from the beginning; she just had to be able to see the first three steps and begin building the bridge. As she progressed further into the project, she could see the next logical steps and in which direction to travel. Also, realizing that these three steps were not the ones that would cause her to accomplish her dream, but were simply steps in building the bridge, Jana felt great relief as the pressure came off to either "make it or fail" instantly. While this is a dramatic departure from the traditional method of goal-setting (seeing a goal and backing into the steps necessary to reach it), it is a fantastic alternate method because it gives people options, especially if they don't know exactly what they are reaching for, or if traditional methods don't work for them.

Every week, Jana accomplished her three goals, then set three new ones for the following week, each of which was achievable in one week's time. One success built upon another, and each new step accomplished led to more steps, as well as more doors opening for Jana. For example, during the very first week, when Jana contacted a voice teacher she had heard about, the teacher told Jana about a piano player who had recently left her band to play at a local country club *who was looking for a singer to join him at the country club bar where he performed on weekends.* This event turned around the direction of Jana's life. She was able to pursue her love of music (and earn some money while learning the ropes) while still holding onto the security of her full-time news job.

While every step did not produce the miracles of this first step, simply performing the steps and moving in the direction of her desired goals brought about successes and opportunities that would never have been available had she not taken that step.

In 1986, Jana decided it was time to leave her current job and actively pursue her dream of becoming a country music singer in Nashville, TN. Jana had previously submitted a tape to a daily talent contest show called "You Can Be A Star". The tape was approved and she was invited to appear on the show. She decided to go to Nashville for her two-week vacation, appear on the show and interview for jobs at the same time, in the event she didn't win the talent contest and its accompanying recording contract.

However, she lacked the money for a two-week hotel stay, so she called area colleges and found one that would rent her a dorm room for $14.00 per night. There was no phone, and the bath was down the hall, but it was within her budget, so she took it.

Not only did Jana have budget limitations, she had a deadline – she had just two weeks to find a job so she could support herself while she tried to break into the music business!

Jana swung into action, setting up interview after interview. Each time she had an interview and got rejected, she would ask for a lead, telling them she only had two weeks to find a job. Everyone she asked for assistance made calls on her behalf to help pave the way. Even if someone told her on the telephone there was nothing available, she'd ask for a five-minute meeting, just to meet and get to know each other, and ask them to point her in the right direction or guide her to someone else they knew. They usually complied.

One important point to note is that Jana believes that neither deadlines nor financial limitations are necessarily bad things. Most people would look upon these factors as obstacles; Jana chose to allow them to spur her on to quicker, more effective action – and it worked! If she had not had financial limitations, she would never have discovered the rented dorm rooms that had no telephones. While the absence of a telephone initially sounds like an obstacle, here's how it played out…

At her first interview at Capitol Records, although she was rejected, she befriended the people there. When they learned of her predicament of trying to get a job without the use of a telephone, they offered her an empty office that contained a telephone she could use for incoming and outgoing calls. They even offered the services of their receptionist to take messages for Jana when she wasn't there! She could call the office and get messages any time during business hours; more importantly, she had a local number to give to interviewers so they could call her. They also gave her tips and leads and often took her out to lunch.

If it weren't for Jana having to rent a dorm room without a telephone, the people at Capitol Records would never have felt the need to help her out by letting her use their empty office, phone and receptionist's services, and…

If it weren't for the people at Capitol Records feeling the need to help her out, Jana would never have become good friends with them, including their receptionist, who became Jana's roommate once Jana moved to Nashville, a move that helped both women keep living expenses low. Not only did this immediately help Jana's financial situation, but Jana's roommate eventually married the Vice President of the record company (coincidentally, the man who had rejected Jana at her first interview), and this man has since become one of Jana's greatest music business mentors and a lifelong friend. By the way, it had been one of his leads that brought her to the job she finally landed at that time (an unadvertised job for a friend of his) working in record promotions as assistant to a woman working out of her condo.

In two weeks, Jana had gone from television reporter to being hired as an assistant for a woman working out of her condo. She was 26 years old (which is the equivalent of being 47 in the music field), but Jana felt she was on her way to reaching her goal, and at least now she was in the music business full-time! Within a year, Jana's new company obtained an office on "music row", where Jana began to develop good working relationships with many people in the business, which created opportunities for her to become known to decision-makers and to showcase her singing and songwriting talents.

For three years Jana tried to get a recording contract with one of the record companies in Nashville. After having been rejected by all the record companies – more than once – and also having been fired from her music business job because her boss felt Jana was too distracted pursuing her own singing career to give 100% to her full-time job, Jana became disillusioned and let all her goal-setting efforts and dreams go. She decided to just "let life happen" for a year, working odd jobs to pay the bills and attending therapy/support groups to keep herself going. She still performed on request, but she had to take a break from her single-minded pursuit of the recording contract.

During these performances-on-request, someone invariably requested a song she had written entitled, "If I Had Only Known." The song was so popular that she usually made a copy of it on a cassette (on her own time) and gave it to the group requesting the performance. She was beginning to spend so much of her time creating this tape with just one song on it that she decided to record a second song on the back and charge a few dollars for it. It worked, and people began to buy her cassettes.

At the end of that year, Jana made a decision that again changed the course of her life. With the success of her single cassettes in mind, she decided to record her "Top 10 Most Rejected Songs", making 100 copies of the tape and offering them for $10.00 each. In her current frame of mind, these 100 copies represented a lifetime supply, but she offered them to friends, family and groups of people who knew and liked her work.

Within one month, she had sold all of them! This gave her $1,000, with which she made 100 more copies. Jana began looking at what kind of effort it would take on her part to sell 100 each month. If she could do that, she could do this for a living without the record companies! Again, Jana's plan worked. Jana has now sold over 100,000 copies of her recordings and has gone on to write and record many more wonderful songs.

In addition, in early 1991, eight members of Reba McEntire's band were tragically killed in a plane crash. In a fortuitous coincidence, the song that had been so popular that it was requested every time Jana performed, the song for which a MasterMind group had been formed by Jana's friends and colleagues who believed it should be on the radio, the song that the record companies *wouldn't record*, "If I Had Only Known", had been put on a reel-to-reel tape by Jana's closest male friend, David Haley of MCA Records, and was played in Ms. McEntire's presence. When she heard Jana's song, she fell in love with it and recorded it as a tribute to her band. It was Jana's first song to make it to the big time.

To top it all off, Jana has now married her "closest male friend"; she and David Haley have been happily married for ten years at the time of this printing.

Through Jana's story, we can see that belief in a dream, persistence toward a goal, and organized and methodic planning, even when you're not sure exactly where you're going and how you're going to get there, will eventually lead to achievement of your dreams – if you don't quit on them. All too often, it would have been easier for Jana to quit on her dream. She could have remained a television news reporter, a career coveted by many, and gotten paid handsomely for it. She could have refused to take an assistant's position in order to break into the music business at the ground floor. And she could have just quit on everything after three years of rejection. But she didn't.

If we see anything in Jana's story, we must see that she doesn't have to wonder "what she would do if she were brave" – she knows.

Part III:

Be An Example

Chapter Twelve

I Don't Know How to Do That

a.k.a. The Power of Personal Examples

I went to college with the intention of going into the field of Psychology. I graduated with a Bachelor of Science degree in Psychology, only to be stopped by the fact that I didn't have the money to go further in my education and couldn't do any form of the counseling I wanted to do without receiving further education and training. (Don't ask me how I got through four years of college without realizing this crucial fact…but I managed it!)

So, I turned to the only thing I knew: I became a secretary. This decision was based partly on the fact that I was an extremely fast and accurate typist. More importantly, this career choice was something that was within my realm of personal experience, so it was not frightening to me. My mother and grandmother were two of the best administrative people I'd ever met. I had real examples of people in my own family who had excelled in administrative positions. I knew of no examples of women in other types of positions in my family. Therefore, I chose the one I knew.

It's eye-opening to realize that, even with my strong will and driving ambition, I had an underlying fear of trying something new. Without a concrete example to follow *in my own personal world*, other careers were completely out of the question for me.

> **Even with a strong will and a desire to succeed, many of us have an underlying fear of trying something new without seeing concrete examples of success *in our own world.***

I realize many people don't need personal examples in their own lives to accomplish goals outside their realm of experience, but I did. I believe there are others like me. This simple lack of a real-life example sometimes makes the accomplishment of a different goal appear so far beyond the realm of possibility that it stops us from believing enough in ourselves and our ingenuity to attempt it. When my goal to be a counselor was halted, I turned to something familiar, something I was comfortable attempting, never even considering other possibilities as options.

If you have personal examples in your lives to encourage and guide you, you have a tremendous opportunity to draw from these examples. Some suggestions are:

1. **Talk to these people**

   Ask them to show you what they do; later, if you're still interested after the initial overview, ask if they'll show you how they do it. Better yet, ask to go with them while they're doing it.

2. **Pick their brains, but be brief.**

   Ask for a set amount of time to chat with them. Have questions prepared, so you don't waste time trying to think of questions to ask when you get there, and then stick to your timetable. If they say no, don't push it. There may be other reasons why they won't, or can't, do it at this time.

3. **Ask if you can help them.**
   Assisting someone else, and having the chance to observe them in action, is an excellent way to learn the ropes of a new task, while helping them in the process. This is also called *apprenticeship*. Don't be afraid to ask! People are flattered when you show an interest in what they do; if they care about you, they'll want to help you learn whether or not it's right for you.

What if I don't have a specific example in my life?

For those who do not see examples of what they'd like to accomplish, look around you – broaden your horizons. There are examples of people who have "been there and done that" for almost any goal you can imagine.

Here are some steps you can take to find the people and information you need to guide you. Once you find these people, follow the steps above in order to learn from them:

1. **Identify what you love to do, as well as career and hobby possibilities contained in those activities.**
   When I established my own household as an adult, I discovered that I loved home decorating and getting ideas I could use in my own home by seeing examples of other nicely decorated homes. I enjoyed all the activities related to touring homes, but never once considered a career in interior design or in real estate (a related field). It wasn't until my real estate agent, who had become a friend, mentioned a career in real estate that a

light eventually came on for me, sparking both a new career idea and the confidence I needed to try it – because I now had a concrete example to whom I could turn for help and guidance.

Ask yourself:

What do I love to do?

Can I make a hobby or career of this activity?

What kind of help or information do I need to determine if I should pursue this? (e.g., initial investment, local opportunities, special classes)

2. **Once you identify what you love to do, look for friends, neighbors, community leaders, colleagues – anyone – in that field, or a related one, and ask them about it.**

Personal examples of people succeeding at what you want to do are EVERYWHERE – if you don't already know one, find one!

Do you know someone in a field related to something you find interesting? If so, talk to him about whether or not he thinks it would be right for you – either as a career or a hobby. He can help you decide. I could have decided against real estate; after all, even though you get to see nice houses, it is a *sales* career – and sales is a tough career choice! Get to know all the good and bad points from someone who knows both sides before making a big change. You don't have to just jump in, but you can at least find out about new possibilities and whether they seem right for you.

If you don't personally know someone who is doing what you want to do, look around you. Examples of people succeeding at what you want to do are EVERYWHERE! All you have to do is look and you'll find them!

Ask yourself:

Who do I know that I can ask for help, guidance and/or assistance?

Who else can I ask for help – local school professors, local business owners, community leaders, a friend of a friend?

Is there more than one person who can talk to me about this?

3. **Do research on the topic of interest to you.**

   While growing up, my husband Bruce experienced debilitating motion sickness on every mode of transportation – cars, buses, trains, planes (which he discovered when he joined the Air Force). When we married, I wanted us to take a cruise, but he was understandably worried about seasickness. He didn't want to ruin our vacation, nor did we want to waste our money on one that didn't work for us.

   However, because I had a strong desire to experience cruising, he was willing to research the topic. We talked to everyone we knew to find out who had experienced cruising and what they had done to avoid seasickness. We then stocked up on seasickness medication, went to a reputable cruise line, booked a cruise on a BIG ship (the least prone to extreme motion, with powerful stabilizers to reduce motion) during *non-hurricane season*, chose the best cabin position (the closer to the center of the ship you go, the less motion) and tried our first cruise. Now we're both hooked! Cruising is our favorite way to vacation, but it never would have been possible without doing the homework that allowed Bruce to feel as comfortable as possible trying something new.

Ask yourself:

Is there a book, magazine or website that specializes in this type of activity?

Are there training classes on this topic – adult education courses, community college, specialty courses?
Who can you ask for help in this area?

Valuable insights may be contained in compliments from others.

4. **Pay attention to encouraging comments from other people.**
   As I previously mentioned, if I hadn't taken the comment from my REALTOR seriously (which I didn't do the first time she said it), I never would have experienced a life-altering change in my thinking and behavior. By listening to what she had to say about my potential abilities, and by allowing her faith in me to give me faith in myself, I opened myself up to a whole new world of opportunity!

   So listen carefully the next time someone tells you that you have a great singing voice, that your cookies are out of this world, or that your help on their computers proved invaluable. There may be valuable information in there that you can use!

Ask yourself:

Who has recently complimented something I've said or done?

What did they compliment?

What do I do extremely well? What do I really enjoy doing?

What do strangers notice first about me – and comment positively on?

The power of mentoring

This concept also illustrates one reason why mentors are so valuable in helping people accomplish their goals, and do it more quickly. Mentors provide real-life examples, step-by-step processes, role-playing and dialogue as well as support and encouragement along the way. They have already "been there and done that" and can help others learn how to succeed, as they have already done.

> **Mentors provide real-life examples, as well as encouragement and guidance, to help others do what they have already done.**

These mentors are not magical or mystical "celebrities" who are so far out of our realm of reality that we can't identify with them. They are real-life people who show us the steps we need to take in order to accomplish what they have already done! They can prevent us from being afraid to take the risks we need to take in order to change an unsatisfying situation, or to venture into a completely new one.

Businesses and sales organizations have come to the realization that mentoring new associates helps them be more successful more quickly because they have the confidence and tools necessary to proceed with the tasks at hand. This situation works, as long as new associates know they are:

- able to observe and learn from an experienced and respected colleague
- confident that their mentor will keep them from making big mistakes
- participating in an established and tested methodology

If any of the above are not true, or if the mentor appears to be too busy, impatient, unwilling or inexperienced for the new associate to learn from him, the relationship (and its subsequent success) breaks down.

By transferring the valuable concept of mentoring, utilized so successfully in the business world, we open ourselves up to new paths for success in our personal lives. By finding people with the right personal experiences and tools, learning from them, asking for guidance to avoid "reinventing the wheel", and then putting our ideas into action with our newly-acquired confidence, we can help ourselves to a whole new world of success in setting and achieving our goals.

Overview

Myths to bust continued:

Myth #1:

If I've never known anyone who has done what I want to do, it will be impossible for me to succeed at it.

Myth #2:

If I don't know what I want to do, no one else will know what I'd be good at, either.

Myth #3:

Successful people are too busy to help others learn their craft.

What myths do I buy into?

___

___

How can I bust them?

___

___

Most common excuses we use to justify our fears and inactivity:

- I don't know how to do that!
- I'll never be given a chance to do that!
- I've never even seen that before. How could I possibly do that?

My "favorite" excuses used to justify my fears and inactivity:

Tips to overcome fear and take action:

1. Even with a strong will and a desire to succeed, many of us have an underlying fear of trying something new without seeing a concrete example of success in our own world.

2. Personal examples of people succeeding at what you want to do are EVERYWHERE – if you don't already know one, look around – you'll find one!

3. Valuable information may be contained in compliments from others.

4. Mentors provide real-life examples, as well as encouragement and guidance, to help others do what they have already done.

Chapter Thirteen

What About the Future?

a.k.a. What Legacy Do You Want to Leave?

Our obligation to our children

Unless we begin focusing on our dreams ourselves, teaching our children at an early age *by our own example* that anyone can achieve his or her dreams, our children will grow up watching us settle for less than we want and deserve.

They will inevitably develop a sense of hopelessness, determining at a young age that there's no use trying for something more because they won't get it anyway – so why bother? If no one in their experience ever gets what they really want anyway, why is it important to make the right decisions on a daily basis? After all, they see millions of unhappy, dissatisfied people doing more complaining about "the way things are" than actively trying to change it. It is our obligation to teach them that even if we can't change the entire world, we can change our own world and our family's world.

Success is a choice. Actually it's a constant string of choices. Whatever our expectations of ourselves and others – whether high or low – we, and everyone around us, recognize them and respond accordingly.

Let's be sure to set our expectations high enough so that not only can we create a better future for ourselves and our world, but we inspire others to follow suit.

Overview

Myths to bust continued:

Myth #1:

We live in such an advanced era that my children will be able to live in a better world, whether I set goals or not.

Myth #2:

My children won't learn any bad behaviors or attitudes from me.

Myth #3:

Nothing I do will change anything. One person can't make a difference in the world.

What myths do I buy into?

____

____

How can I bust them?

____

____

Most common excuses we use to justify our fears and inactivity:

- No one I know sets goals, so I don't have to do that, either!
- My children don't listen to me, anyway.
- No one listens to me!
- I'm not anybody's role model, so I can just do what I want to do
- I don't want to be anybody's role model. Whoever said I had to be a role model?
- My parents never set goals, and I turned out OK. So, I don't need to set goals, either. My kids will be just fine!
- One little action on my part won't change a darn thing – so why bother trying!
- That problem is too big – we can't solve it!
- I can't solve the problems of the world!

My "favorite" excuses used to justify my fears and inactivity:

Tips to overcome fear and take action:

1. Begin making YOUR world a little better. Take small actions that your children (and others) can see. Allow them to see you set goals and succeed. Don't let the only thing they learn from you and others around you be that no one ever achieves their goals, so they shouldn't bother trying.

2. Set small goals with your children, so they can participate in the feeling of accomplish from an early age. Keeping their rooms clean, getting good grades, passing a difficult exam are all great goals to set and then celebrate when they're accomplished!

3. Research and point out to your children individuals who have made a difference – not only in the world as a whole, but in your own individual world (a parent, a sibling, a friend who has helped you or taught you valuable lessons). Show your children and your friends' children that small accomplishments are reasons to celebrate. Teach them that they also lead to big accomplishments.

Now that you've uncovered the mindsets and habits necessary for (as well as the obstacles to) achieving your dreams, order Sandy's Life Plan and let her show you HOW to achieve them!

Complete with instructions and forms for step-by-step planning and budgeting, identifying your specific dreams and goals, creating action items, and monitoring them on a regularly basis, your own personal Life Plan will set you firmly on the path to achieving all your personal and professional dreams.

Sandy Geroux

speaker, trainer, author, coach

Order Sandy's Life Plan Today!

Product Name	Product Description	Price	Qty	Total
Life Plan Workbook & CD	Printed workbook and CD of forms/templates to create and monitor your own Life Plan for higher achievement toward your personal and professional dreams!	$14.99		
No Risk, No Reward Mem-Cards	Deck of 27 flash cards on the absolute necessity and benefit of taking reasonable and appropriate risks in business and in life! Complete with mindsets, tips and inspiring quotations to reinforce the message.	$10.00		
		Shipping		$5.00
		6.5% FL Tax (if FL resident)		
		TOTAL		

If you'd like to order multiple copies of Sandy's book for your organization, or book her to speak at your next event, please call us for volume pricing and/or speaking availability at 1-866-954-2277 (toll-free) or (407) 856-1188 (local Orlando, FL)

Three Easy Ways To Order!

1. *Fax this order form, TOLL-FREE, to* ***1-866-315-2277*** *today!*
2. *Call, TOLL-FREE,* ***1-866-954-2277*** *to order by phone. Please have your credit card ready when calling.*
3. *Go online at www.sandygeroux.com and order it, along with Sandy's other motivational success tools, through our online store!*

Name ______________________________
Address ______________________________
City ____________________ State ________ Zip ________
Phone (   ) E-mail: ____________________

❑ My check or money order, made out to ICAPS, is enclosed.
❑ Visa ❑ MasterCard ❑ American Express ❑ Discover

Card number ____________________ Expires________
Cardholder's Name______________________________
Signature ______________________________

Geroux Performance Group

1-866-954-2277 Phone (toll-free)
1-866-315-2277 Fax (toll-free)
e-mail: sandyg@sandygeroux.com
www.sandygeroux.com